INVESTOR'S RIGHTS HANDBOOK

Stocks
Bonds
Mutual Funds
Other Securities Investments

Practising Law Institute Guides

ESTATE PLANNING
How to Preserve Your Estate for Your Loved Ones
by Jerome A. Manning

INVESTOR'S RIGHTS HANDBOOK
• Stocks • Bonds • Mutual Funds
• Other Securities Investments
by Larry D. Soderquist

YOUR RIGHTS IN THE WORKPLACE
Everything Employees Need to Know
by Henry H. Perritt, Jr.

PERSONAL BANKRUPTCY
What Every Debtor and Creditor Needs to Know
by William C. Hillman

A Practising Law Institute Guide

INVESTOR'S RIGHTS HANDBOOK

Stocks
Bonds
Mutual Funds
Other Securities Investments

LARRY D. SODERQUIST

Practising Law Institute
NEW YORK

I am grateful to the many people who helped with this book. I especially want to thank Margaret D. Anagnos, Michael J. McSunas, Andrea R. Reichel, Laura A. Rost, and Jonathan A. Shayne for their very helpful research assistance, including in the case of Jon Shayne his valuable comments on and checking of numerous details in the manuscript. For his splendid editorial work on the book, I also want especially to thank Henry W. Enberg II.

Larry D. Soderquist

Library of Congress Catalog Card Number: 93-084181
ISBN: 0-87224-050-9

Contents

v

Contents

Contents

This Book Is About . . .

This book is about protecting your rights as an investor in stocks, bonds, mutual fund shares, and other kinds of securities. The most important thing to know is that **the best time to protect your rights is at the beginning of a transaction**. It's a good thing to be able to win your rights after an investment has gone sour, but it's far better to plan your investment relationships and set up your transactions so that your rights are secure from the start.

With that in mind, this book will help you operate as an investor at all the critical points: as you establish investment relationships, as you make investments, and as you live with investments. It will help you spot problems with investments and tell you how you can fight back if you have been cheated or are the victim of a mistake.

What this book does is allow you to keep a securities lawyer on call, available at any time you want, to answer your questions about investing. You might ask why you would want to have questions answered by a securities lawyer. After all, there is an image abroad that securities law-

1

yers put together giant mergers, fight battles for corporate control, and set up complex schemes to entrench management at the expense of the shareholders. That isn't your world. It isn't the world of most securities lawyers either.

A securities lawyer is someone who works with the laws and regulations that govern "securities." The most common securities are what I mentioned above, stocks, bonds, shares in mutual funds, and the like. There are federal and state laws that govern the purchase and sale of securities, and there are general laws (on contracts, fraud, and sales, for example) that apply to securities as well as to other forms of property. Securities lawyers can be found on both sides of disputes on all these matters.

Some of the questions this book answers are purely legal, such as:

- Are there estate tax consequences from having a joint brokerage account?
- What has to be shown in order to prove churning of a brokerage account? ("Churning" is one of the most common scams crooked brokers pull, and this book will tell you just what it is and how to defend yourself against it.)

Other questions depend on a blend of legal, business, and practical considerations for their answers, such as:

- Are there clauses I should cross out in the client agreement with my brokerage firm?
- When might a broker call me with a recommendation that is both legal and very close to a sure thing?

- What happens if one of my stock certificates is lost or stolen?
- What are the ten most common ways investors are cheated?
- What can I do if I feel cheated in an investment or victimized by a broker's or brokerage firm's mistake?

Many questions are business or practical questions answered from a securities lawyer's point of view, such as:

- Should I consider a discretionary account?
- What should I ask a broker about a buy recommendation?
- Can pyramid schemes make money for investors?

I have divided this book into the four stages of investing: getting started, investing, living with the investment, and solving your problems with your investment. Then I have collected some of the terms you need to know as an investor. Finally, there is an index so you can find the particular answer you need. The titles of the parts are:

- Getting Set with Investment Professionals
- Making Investments
- Living with Investments
- Scams, Swindles, Frauds, and Plain Mistakes (and How to Fight Back)
- What Does . . . Mean?
- Index

When you have questions you'd like to ask a securities lawyer, just pull this book off your shelf. While no book can give you professional legal advice, this book can and will give you a large amount of the information you need to make the right decisions as an investor. It also will help you decide when you need to talk to a lawyer, and it will help you choose the right one.

Part I

GETTING SET WITH INVESTMENT PROFESSIONALS

There are successful investors who work entirely on their own, trusting their own ability to set priorities, to research opportunities, and to make the tough decisions of what to buy and sell. Most investors, however, need help. They lack the time or interest to track the market carefully and want to be able to turn to an investment professional. For the investor who needs help, the first question is not, "Who can help me?"; it's, "What kind of help do I need?" There are different types of investment professions. An investor must decide, therefore, what type of help — what profession — he or she needs before looking for the right person — the right professional.

In the next few pages, we'll look at the various kinds of help investment professionals offer, and answer some of the typical questions that arise for investors as they set up investment relationships. We'll cover financial planners (chapter 1) and investment advisers (chapter 2) and brokers and brokerage firms (chapter 3). Chapter 3 is particularly important in this part of the book because it examines how you establish yourself as a client of a brokerage firm, and how you can avoid some serious pitfalls of that relationship.

CHAPTER

1

Financial Planners

What is a financial planner?

A financial planner is someone who develops financial plans. I can't be more precise because there aren't many rules to the game of financial planning, but I can try to show what a financial plan is and why you would want someone to develop one for you.

What is a financial plan?

Basically, a financial plan lists where you expect to get your funds from and what you expect to do with them. The kind we are concerned with differs from the garden-variety household budget in that it focuses on what can be done with funds available for investment. Even more basically, the plan should indicate whether you can afford to invest anything.

The typical plan takes into account your assets, your income, and your family's circumstances, and sets your investment goals. It often covers various investment vehicles, such as bank accounts, insurance policies, pension funds, stocks, bonds, and mutual funds, and suggests which you should use and how much you should put in each. The type and amount of investments suggested by a financial planner tend to be influenced heavily by the background of the planner and by what kind of investments, if any, the planner gets fees for selling.

What kind of people tend to be financial planners?

You name it. A lot of financial planners have sold insurance or been stockbrokers; many combine those professions with financial planning. Some other backgrounds of financial planners are accounting, law, banking, and real estate brokerage. Others come from any background you can imagine.

Are there legal requirements for being a financial planner?

There are no licensing or other requirements for being a "financial planner," at least on the national level. Depending on various factors, however, a financial planner likely will have to register as an investment adviser. He or she also may need to be licensed as a stockbroker.

If someone claims to be a "financial planner," what does that say about his or her training?

As far as the federal government is concerned, nothing. There is no particular training someone must have to use the title "financial planner."

Some financial planners have completed a series of courses and passed certain qualifying examinations given by the College of Financial Planning, which is located in Denver, Colorado, and been certified by the college as

Certified Financial Planners. That entitles them to use the letters "CFP" after their names. Along the same lines, some insurance agents complete a series of courses and pass examinations that allow them to call themselves Chartered Financial Consultants and to use the letters "ChFC" after their names. It is fair to say that both Certified Financial Planners and Chartered Financial Consultants have been trained as financial planners.

Are people sporting CFPs and ChFCs the only persons who have had training as financial planners?

No. It is certainly true that many people who hold degrees in business have been trained in what might be called "financial planning," and it is also true that many insurance agents and stockbrokers have received that training, either formally or through their employment.

Does an investor need a financial planner?

No, but every investor very definitely needs a financial plan. Some investors want to do all their own financial planning, but that's not as easy as it may sound. A good financial planner may be able to tell an investor in a few minutes things that would take the investor months to learn on his or her own. The average investor will do an awful lot of "reinventing the wheel" in the course of learning about financial planning.

We'll talk a little bit about fees later, but for now it can be said that if an investor has only a small amount to invest, hiring a financial planner may not be economically feasible. In that case, or if for some other reason an investor wants to do his or her own financial planning, the best thing to do is go to a bookstore and buy a book on the subject. That way, it may be possible to cut the wasted effort down to reinventing the hubcap.

Why all this folderol; can't the typical investor figure out somehow that 6 percent beats 5 percent?

Good financial planners operate on the basis of a lot of experience, either their own or the experience that's crystallized in the books they've read and the courses they've taken. Experience teaches, for example, that an investor of a certain age with a family of a certain size and income in a certain range would be wise to provide a certain type and amount of life insurance and to set aside a certain percentage of assets as an emergency fund before even thinking about returns on investments.

A good financial planner will take those kinds of considerations, and a whole lot more, into account, along with the investor's obvious desire to maximize return on a particular kind of investment.

What fee should you expect to pay a financial planner?

Financial planners tend to work in one of three ways:

1. Some work for straight fees. These may be flat fees, hourly fees, or fees based on some other standard, such as the amounts involved in the plan.

2. Some financial planners receive only commissions based on financial products they sell. Typical examples are commissions from life insurance and fees from the sale of stocks or mutual funds.

3. Some financial planners receive a combination of fees and commissions, or sometimes a set fee that is decreased by the amount of commissions earned on whatever financial products the investor buys from the planner.

Doesn't the fee arrangement tend to influence the financial plan?

Absolutely. Not only is it virtually impossible for the average person, financial planners included, to choose disinterestedly between an investment vehicle that earns a commission and one that doesn't, even the most honest and scrupulous planner faces the unconscious bias inherent in choosing between the investment vehicle to which the planner has devoted his or her career and some other vehicle that might be better for the client.

Does that mean an investor should choose only a financial planner who gets a straight fee?

Life's not that simple. Other things being equal, going to a "fee-only" planner would usually make the most sense. Other things are rarely equal in the real world, however. It may well be true that the best planner available for a particular investor is someone whose main job is selling insurance or stocks. The point, though, is that if commissions to the financial planner may be involved in the financial plan, the investor must evaluate the plan with that fact in mind.

In that regard, the investor needs to look not only at the type of investments the planner suggests, but at the relative price of the investments when purchased through the planner and when purchased through someone else.

For example, a suggestion by a financial planner that the investor purchase $300,000 of life insurance may be excellent advice. That does not mean, however, that it would necessarily make good financial sense to buy life insurance through the planner's company. The cost of virtually identical insurance varies greatly from insurance company to insurance company, and nowhere is it written that the financial planner's company must be the low-cost provider.

If an investor does go to a "fee-only" financial planner, what fee should be expected?

I'm sure there are so-called financial planners who will do what purports to be a plan for $50. What you will probably get from them is a computer printout generated by a software program into which the "planner" has entered some basic financial data provided by you. Depending on the software, the plan may even be worth $50, but I wouldn't bank on it. Beyond that, an investor should probably expect fees of at least $300-$400 for a simple plan and up to several thousand dollars for a complex one. In a sense, an investor is likely to get the financial plan he or she pays for. While it is true that an investor can spend a lot of money for a worthless plan, he or she is not likely to get a very useful plan for near nothing.

With those preliminaries out of the way, how do I choose a financial planner?

I wish there were an easy answer to this one. The first thing to do is ask people with experience. These might be people who have used a financial planner or people like lawyers, accountants, or stockbrokers who have had the opportunity to evaluate plans prepared by various financial planners. We've discussed how the planner will be paid. The planner's credentials are certainly also important. It is a positive sign if the planner is a Certified Financial Planner or a Chartered Financial Consultant, but some planners holding those titles aren't worth anything as planners and some people without any formal training are highly gifted.

Expertise is where you find it, so anything that tells you about real expertise (for example, recommendations by knowledgeable people) is more important than paper credentials. Beyond recommendations and credentials, you are basically left to follow your own intuition after meeting and talking to the prospective planner.

One thing to keep firmly in mind is that no matter how much confidence an investor has in a planner at the beginning of the process, the investor needs to evaluate the finished plan carefully. The investor also needs to evaluate the job the planner is doing throughout the course of the planning relationship.

What does an investor need to look for in the financial planner while the plan is being developed?

You must listen to the questions the planner is asking. Without asking a lot of questions, a planner cannot possibly develop a good, individualized plan. If the information-gathering session is short and painless, think two or three times about the ability of the planner. No pain, no gain.

How can an investor evaluate the finished plan?

Obviously, an investor who can evaluate the financial plan fully and with a high degree of sophistication probably did not need the planner in the first place. Certainly, the investor can apply good common sense and ask questions, and keep asking questions, until the investor is satisfied that the planner knew what he or she was doing. Don't put a financial plan into effect until you are satisfied that it makes good sense.

Could you be more specific?

Ask yourself, "Does the plan take account of my situation? Is it pointed in the direction I want to go?" For example, assume you work but your spouse doesn't and you don't have any substantial assets. Your first need is financial security, and that almost always means substantial life and disability insurance; if that type of insurance is not in the plan, something is very wrong.

Another example relates to risk tolerance. Some people love taking risks and want a financial plan that offers them the maximum opportunity for return, no matter how high the risk. A good financial planner might suggest that a reasonable portion of such an investor's capital be put into, say, commodities futures. On the other hand, another person with an otherwise equal situation may not be able to sleep at night if he or she has to worry about the possibility of losing money on an investment. Instead of commodities futures, the planner may need to suggest government bonds to that investor.

Should tax planning be part of the financial plan?

Absolutely, and good financial planners do take taxes into account while drawing their plan. Obviously, a financial planner who is also an accountant or a tax lawyer is more likely to do sophisticated tax planning than the average planner.

Are there expiration dates on financial plans?

I'd answer that with a firm yes and no. If the plan fits your needs at first and your needs stay the same, it could be good for the long haul. On the other hand, changes in the national or world economy or in the tax laws or the financial markets may require immediate, far-reaching changes in your financial plan.

Certainly a plan needs to be changed as an investor's circumstances or goals change. A good financial planner should give an investor advice about monitoring the plan, but in any case the investor should monitor it on his or her own. An investor should expect any plan to need modification as the years go by, if for no other reason than that the investor will go through various phases of life. A plan typically would be quite different for a young investor looking toward putting children through college and the same investor later looking forward to retirement.

What are the major dangers from financial planners? How can you avoid disaster?

There are lots of investment scams around, and crooks can call themselves "financial planners" as easily as anything else. Perhaps especially to be looked out for is a financial planner who wants not only to suggest, but to sell you, some investment scheme that promises an unusually high return. The old wisdom holds: if something is too good to be true, it ain't true.

CHAPTER

2

Investment Advisers

What is an investment adviser?

Once you have a financial plan in hand, whether developed by a planner or homegrown, you come to the investment adviser (who could be your financial planner wearing a different hat). There are various types of investment advisers, but the kind we are talking about in this book have one thing in common: they all either (1) make specific recommendations on what securities to buy and sell or (2) buy and sell the securities for you. If your financial plan suggests that you put 20 percent of your assets in common stocks, the investment adviser would pick the stocks. Some investment advisers merely publish weekly or monthly newsletters for their clients. Most, however, work in one way or the other with investors more directly. Another term used to describe investment advisers is "money managers."

Do investment advisers work in offices of their own, or for some company?

Some investment advisers work entirely on their own, some work in investment advisory firms, some work for brokerage houses, some in bank trust departments, and some for other financial institutions.

Do I have to turn over all of my investment decisions if I hire an investment adviser?

No, but it is typical for investment advisers to make investment decisions for all funds that are turned over to them, with the idea being that they will make those decisions within the confines of a financial plan. In some situations, however, the investment adviser merely suggests buy and sell decisions to the investor.

If I turn money over to an investment adviser, will he or she manage my money in a single fund or will it be thrown in with other investors' funds and managed all together?

Let's be realistic: although investment advisers work in each of those ways, unless we're talking big money, individual investment management is unlikely. It simply is not economically feasible for an investment adviser to make individualized decisions unless a lot of money is involved. If, however, the investment objectives are the same for a number of clients, an investment adviser can do an equally good job for each of them by pooling their funds and managing all the funds together. Bank trust departments, for example, often manage pooled accounts for a large number of clients.

How much do the services of an investment adviser cost?

The fees of investment advisers vary with the kind of accounts managed. A bank trust department may charge an annual fee of only one-half of one percent of the funds under management for a pooled account, whereas an investment adviser managing an individual fund may charge an annual fee of 1 or 2 percent. On top of that, the investor would be responsible for brokerage fees. Alternatively, brokerage firms sometimes offer so-called wrap fees, covering both investment advice and brokerage fees. A typical wrap fee would be 3 percent a year of the funds under management.

Is there a minimum dollar amount necessary for getting investment advisory services?

Yes, but it varies from investment adviser to investment adviser; $100,000 is common.

How individualized will investment advisory services be if an investor has $100,000 to invest?

While some investment advisers would probably give such an account completely individualized attention, most would not, and neither should an investor necessarily want them to. A great many of an investment adviser's clients will have approximately the same objectives, and the adviser, as a practical matter, can have in mind at any given time only a limited number of investments that he or she thinks are superior. It stands to reason, therefore, that an investment adviser would make the same buy and sell decisions for a number of clients. In that circumstance, of course, each individual investor has a right to expect that the adviser will at all times keep that investor's particular situation in mind to the extent it is necessary.

Are there any educational or other requirements before someone can use the title "investment adviser"?

Insofar as federal regulation is concerned, anyone can claim to be an investment adviser. Obviously, however, investment advisory firms, brokerage firms, and banks are unlikely to hire people as investment advisers unless those doing the hiring have confidence in the employee's ability, typically because of education or experience. It might be added here that there is an Institute of Chartered Financial Analysts, headquartered in Charlottesville, Virginia, that gives examinations to individuals who wish to be able to call themselves Chartered Financial Analysts. These people typically use the initials CFA after their names.

Is there any federal or state regulation of investment advisers?

With some exceptions, investment advisers are required to register under a federal statute, the Investment Advisers Act of 1940. (Very incidentally, the spelling of the name of that Act is the reason many securities lawyers are so careful never to call anyone an "advisor.") The Act requires investment advisers to make certain disclosures to the Securities and Exchange Commission and to clients. There are some exceptions to the registration requirement. For example, stockbrokers typically are not required to register as investment advisers, it being understood that ordinary stockbrokers, who must be licensed under another federal statute, often provide investment advice as part of their job. Many states also regulate the activities of investment advisers to one extent or another.

How can I tell if I need an investment adviser?

Assuming you have enough funds to invest so that it is possible and practical to have an investment adviser, the decision whether to have one is highly personal. One issue, of course, is your ability to handle your own investment decisions. Another issue is the time and energy you have available for looking after investments, and whether doing so gives pleasure or constitutes drudgery. Yet another important issue is how comfortable you are in turning investment decision over to someone else. Some investors could not sleep at night knowing their money was in someone else's hands, while others want to turn investment decisions over to professionals precisely so that they can get to sleep at night.

How does one find a good investment adviser?

There is no simple way to find a good investment adviser. Recommendations from other investors, or from lawyers or accountants who have seen the results of various investment advisers' work, are good sources of recommendations.

Obviously, track record is critically important, and an investor should ask a prospective adviser a lot of questions about past performance. In doing so, remember that if the stock market has been going up steadily for a time, it will not have taken a financial genius to have made money for clients. One good thing to do is compare the adviser's record of investing against broad market indices to see if the adviser has been beating the market.

Beyond any objective criteria for choosing an investment adviser, it is important that the investor have a strong general feeling of confidence in the adviser. One of the benefits of turning one's money over to a professional manager is that an investor does not then have to worry about investment decisions. But, no matter what credentials and track record an investment adviser has, the investor cannot help worrying about investment decisions if he or she does not have confidence in the adviser.

If an investor does not have sufficient funds to make having an investment adviser a real option, how can the investor still get professional management?

One way to get professional management for one's investments is to buy shares in a mutual fund. The funds have their own money managers, and there is no shortage of mutual funds from which to choose. We'll discuss mutual funds in chapter 4.

Say I want to choose an investment advisory newsletter. How do I find a good one?

That's not an easy question, because there are a great many such newsletters to choose from. In addition to the issue of whether a particular newsletter covers the basic type of investment you have in mind, one thing you would like to know, of course, is how successful a newsletter has been in the past at choosing securities to buy and sell. Financial magazines sometimes discuss how well various newsletters have done, and there are one or more specialized publications that report on the performance of investment advisory newsletters. By studying a library's file of back issues of financial magazines, and of whatever other publications you may have found, you may fairly quickly discover one or more newsletters that have consistently made successful predictions in years past. Ask the research librarian for help if you aren't up to speed on the *Reader's Guide to Periodical Literature* and the various computer databases that can be searched, in addition to the plain old card catalogue. (For this and other library visits suggested in this book, you may want to see if you can use the library of a business school near you, especially if you don't find everything you want in your public library.) Remember, as you do your research, that success by a newsletter in the past does not guarantee success in the future.

How much should I expect to pay for a newsletter?

Investment advisory newsletters are expensive. Expect to pay in excess of $100 per year, and don't be surprised if the cost is some hundreds of dollars a year.

CHAPTER

3

Brokerage Firms

What is a brokerage firm?

For the ordinary investor, a brokerage firm is the company that helps him or her buy and sell securities. The whole story is much more complicated than that, because brokerage firms perform many functions and operate in many ways. Complicating the matter further is the fact that people use several terms to refer to these firms. Sometimes one hears them called investment banks or, more usually, investment banking firms. These are simply fancier terms that mean the same thing as "brokerage firm." The firms also are often referred to as securities firms.

MARKET FUNCTIONS OF BROKERAGE FIRMS

What is a broker?

The word "broker" means different things in different contexts. To a brokerage firm, the firm is a broker when it helps investors buy and sell securities that are owned by someone other than the firm. The term also is commonly used to refer to the person within the brokerage firm with whom investors deal. In legal language, that person is referred to as a "registered representative," while the brokerage firm probably calls him or her something like "account executive."

The stock exchanges are basically auction markets, and when an investor wants to buy securities that are listed on an exchange, the investor's brokerage firm acts as a broker in helping the investor buy or sell the securities on the exchange.

What is a dealer?

In the language of the securities industry, the term "dealer" refers to a brokerage firm when it buys and sells securities for its own account, taking title itself when it buys securities from an investor and passing title to an investor when it sells. The over-the-counter market (which simply means the market for securities that are not traded on an exchange) is not an auction market. In the over-the-counter market, securities firms operate as dealers when they buy and sell securities for their own accounts. It might be added here that the term "dealer" is used more broadly in the federal securities laws, where it includes both brokers and dealers as we have described them here.

What is a market maker?

A market maker is a dealer, operating in the over-the-counter market, that maintains an inventory of a particular company's securities and holds itself out as being willing, on a continuing basis, to buy and sell those securities. If an investor goes to a brokerage firm to buy an over-the-counter security, and the firm is not a market maker in that security, the brokerage firm will merely help the investor purchase the security from another brokerage firm. In that case, the investor's brokerage firm will act as a broker.

What is an underwriter?

For our purposes, an "underwriter" is a securities firm that helps a company, or its major shareholders, sell securities to the public through an offering that is registered under the federal securities laws. (Incidentally, "shareholder" means the same as "stockholder.") In a registered offering, the sellers contract with a number of securities firms that will act as underwriters, typically buying the securities at one price and then immediately attempting to resale them to the public at a higher price.

From an investor's standpoint, buying securities in such an offering is somewhat different from buying securities on a stock exchange or in the over-the-counter market. In an underwritten offering, the securities firm will not charge a commission for doing the transaction, because the firm is getting its compensation from selling the securities at a higher price than it bought them for. Also, in a registered public offering, the investor will be provided a prospectus that describes the company and the offering. We'll discuss the prospectus at greater length later.

Complicating the matter somewhat is the fact that underwriters often sell some of their securities not to the public, but to other securities firms, which then resell the securities to the public. In that case, the other securities firms are operating as dealers. Also complicating the matter is the fact that, under the securities laws, the term "underwriter" is defined much more broadly than it is in common usage. In fact, it is possible for individuals to find themselves denominated underwriters, usually with unhappy consequences.

TYPES OF BROKERAGE FIRMS

What are the various types of brokerage firms?

There are various ways to break down brokerage firms into different categories. First, one can differentiate among full-service, specialized, and discount firms. Then one can differentiate between retail and nonretail firms. Finally one can differentiate between national and regional firms.

What is a full-service firm?

As the name implies, a full-service brokerage firm provides all the services typically offered by brokerage firms. Such firms will act for investors buying and selling any type of security (such as stocks, corporate and government bonds, mutual fund shares, and limited partnership interests) and typically any type of commodity contract (from gold to frozen pork bellies). The firms also offer money market accounts (in which one can park funds for the short term at favorable interest rates), often coupled with checking accounts. Full-service firms also offer investment advisory services, whereby they will manage one's investments for a fee. Such firms also typically operate as underwriters and dealers to help companies and their major shareholders sell securities to the public, and they provide financial advice to companies that may wish to sell securities. So far as the individual investor is concerned, one of the most important functions of the full-service firm is its research and analysis of various companies and its provision of reports and recommendations to its customers.

What is a specialized firm?

Specialized firms are brokerage firms that provide more or less full services, but with respect to only some kinds of securities. The most common example is a firm that deals only in municipal bonds.

What is a discount firm?

Discount brokerage firms are the exact opposite of full-service firms. Discount firms do nothing more, or little more, than buy and sell securities for customers. They do not have research departments and, therefore, save the substantial amount of money it takes to staff such departments. Not only do such firms not have analysts, neither are their sales personnel expected to do any more for customers than take buy and sell orders, whereas in full-service firms sales people spend much of their time discussing possible investments with customers. As a result of their offering very limited services, discount firms can afford to charge very much lower commissions than full-service firms. Commissions vary, among both full-service and discount firms, by type and amount of securities being purchased, and commissions also fluctuate over time.

To give an idea, however, of the difference between commissions charged by full-service and discount firms, it would not be unusual for a discount firm to charge substantially less than half the commission of a full-service firm.

What is a retail firm?

Retail brokerage firms are the firms that the average investor is likely to be most familiar with, since these are the firms that have storefront offices and that advertise for business from the general public. In the securities business, these firms are often referred to as wire houses, which term came from the idea that the firm would have offices spread all over the country connected by telephone, Telex, and other communications lines. Merrill Lynch, Pierce, Fenner & Smith Inc. is the best known wire house.

How do nonretail firms differ from retail ones?

Nonretail securities firms do not do a retail business, but rather they sell securities mostly to institutions, such as insurance companies and pension funds, or they wholesale securities to retail firms. In addition, nonretail firms typically service a fairly small number of wealthy individual investors. You might hear a nonretail firm referred to as an institutional firm.

How do national and regional securities firms differ?

In addition to the obvious — a differing geographical spread of their offices — regional firms often develop special expertise in securities issued by companies in their region.

CHOOSING A BROKER

What should I focus on in choosing a brokerage firm?

Typically it should make little difference to the ordinary investor whether the firm chosen is national or regional, and only retail firms will be available. The big question, therefore, is whether the investor should go with a full-service or a discount firm.

How do I choose between a full-service and a discount brokerage firm?

In one sense the answer to this question is simple: if you don't need the research, analysis, and investment advice a full-service firm offers, you should go with a discount firm. The underlying question, whether you need those services, is more difficult. If you have hired an investment adviser to make buy-and-sell recommendations, and if your deal with the adviser is that you will effect your own trades, then you certainly should work through a discount firm.

Also, if you have decided to do your own research and analysis, and make buy-and-sell decisions personally, the choice of a discount firm is clear. Otherwise, an investor pretty much needs the recommendations that only a full-service firm can provide.

Just what kind of investment advice does a full-service firm provide?

Most of the investment advice an investor receives from a full-service firm comes ultimately from the firm's research department, which writes reports on various industries and companies. Those reports can be obtained through your broker, whose opinions should also be informed by the findings of the research department. If you call your broker to ask about a particular company, the broker should be able to check what the research department recommends with respect to that company's stock. Also, brokers often call investors with the firm's buy or sell recommendations. Sometimes, of course, the broker comes up with recommendations on his or her own.

How important should an investor consider a full-service firm's investment advice to be?

That's impossible to answer in general, because investors vary so greatly. In seeking an answer to that question, an investor should consider one thing that may not be apparent on the surface. That is, how important it will be to you to have someone calling with recommendations, and how important it will be for you to be able to call someone and discuss a possible investment decision? The answer to those questions depends somewhat on your background, knowledge, and skills, but it also relates to your basic personality and desires. It might help to think about the question this way: suppose you read in the paper that a company you own stock in has just announced a loss for its last quarter. Suppose further that that raises the question in your mind whether you should sell the stock. Are you the kind of person who wants to make that decision on his on her own, or would you like to call a broker and discuss the issue, and perhaps get information from a research department report on the stock?

Suppose I decide to use a full-service firm. How do I choose one?

There are differences in firms, and so far as you are concerned, the most important of those differences is the quality of the firm's research department. It is very difficult, however, for an investor to compare firms and make good decisions about their differences. One thing that might help is a trip to the public library and a little research into articles in financial magazines that compare firms. In general, however, I think it is more important to try to choose the right broker than it is to attempt to choose the best firm.

How do I find the right broker?

The best starting place is a recommendation from someone whose judgment you trust. In seeking a recommendation, you have to ask some specific questions designed to get at the issue of whether a broker will be right for you. For example, you need to find out if a person recommending his or her own broker has somewhat the same financial position and investment objectives that you have. Also, don't just ask whether the recommender is happy with the broker. Rather, ask such questions as

* How often does the broker call you with recommendations?

- What does the broker do when you ask questions about specific stocks?
- How available is the broker for telephone calls?
- How good have the broker's recommendations turned out to be?
- Does the broker always execute your buy-and-sell orders promptly and without problems?
- Does the broker ever pressure you when you don't want to follow a recommendation?
- Is there any question whatever about the broker's integrity? (You can, by the way, request information on discipline and other problems involving a broker, or a brokerage firm, by calling the National Association of Securities Dealers, Inc., at [800] 289-9999; information will be mailed to you.)

After I have collected recommendations, how should I proceed from there?

Pick the one or two brokers who sound best to you, call them on the telephone, and make appointments to visit them. At the meeting, try to figure out your own answers to the kinds of questions above. Talk to the brokers about their experience, but be open to dealing with a relatively inexperienced broker if he or she fits the bill for you in other ways. Sometimes a fairly new broker will make up for a relative lack of experience with an extra measure of energy and interest.

Ask questions that help you form your own opinion as to whether the broker will be interested in handling your account the way you want it handled. For example, if you want lots of recommendations, will you get them?

On the same lines, if you don't want a lot of recommendations, will you get them anyway? Be alert to pick up clues about the broker's basic integrity. Are the broker's answers forthright? Does he or she know how to say, "I don't know"? Make sure the personality fit between you and a prospective broker is good. That is extremely important, and no one can gauge it except you.

What kind of training can I expect a broker to have?

There is no particular background that brokers share. It is important for you to know that brokers are mainly sales personnel, and as such they are likely to have more in common with other people who sell than they have with the business managers or analysts in their own brokerage firm.

Do brokerage firms provide their own training to brokers?

Yes they do, although it varies greatly from firm to firm. Again you should realize, however, that that training will be designed to make the person better at selling securities than at picking good stocks to buy and sell. That is not necessarily bad, because brokerage firms expect most buy-and-sell recommendations to come from their research departments.

All firms provide basic training in the laws and regulations that govern brokers, that is, in federal and state securities laws and regulations, and also in the rules of the various stock exchanges and of the National Association of Securities Dealers, Inc. (the NASD). The NASD is an association to which virtually all brokerage firms belong, and which has power, under federal law, to regulate the activities of brokerage firms and the brokers who work for them. In the language of the statute, it is a self-regulatory organization, or SRO.

Are brokers licensed, and can they lose their license for misbehavior?

Yes, brokers have to take a test prepared by the NASD and various exchanges, and, after passing that test, they can become licensed under federal law. They can lose their license if they fail to follow the laws and regulations that govern brokers' conduct. States have their own licensing requirements.

What if I can't come up with a good recommendation for a broker?

In that case I would suggest you pick the one, two, or three firms in your area that you believe would be best for you. Call the offices of those firms that are most convenient to you, and ask to speak to the branch manager. Tell the manager that you would like to talk with a broker about opening an account, and also tell the manager how much money you have to invest and what your basic objectives are. The manager will be happy to suggest a broker.

Of course, the manager may merely suggest the broker who has the fewest customers. It may help to tell the manager up front that you're calling because you want his or her good advice and that you don't want merely to be sent to the least busy broker.

In any case, however, once you meet with the suggested broker you will have a chance to form your own opinion based on an interview. Unless you are really sold on the first broker you talk with, I would suggest that you go through the procedure with more than one brokerage firm before making a decision on a broker. Also, consider any decision you make at this point to be tentative, because it likely will be impossible to tell after only a short interview whether the broker will in fact be right for you.

Are there any things that I should particularly watch out for when interviewing brokers?

Yes, integrity. Be especially wary of a broker who promises too much. If a prospective broker "guarantees" to make you money in anything but the most conservative investments, get up and run.

OPENING A BROKERAGE ACCOUNT

Once I've settled on a broker, where do we go from there?

The first thing you need to do is open an account. There are two basic kinds of accounts, cash accounts and margin accounts. A cash account requires that you pay for most securities purchased within five business days. In a margin account, the brokerage firm extends you credit, so that you can buy stocks partially on credit.

Information Required

What is involved in setting up an account?

You will have to answer some questions the broker will put to you and fill out and sign one or more forms. The questioning should be rather intrusive, but you shouldn't be put off by it. Generally, the more your broker knows about you the better; good brokerage firms would want a good bit of information as a matter of business practice. Further, they are required to seek information in any case. The New York Stock Exchange and the NASD have "Know Your Customer" rules.

What kind of information will be required of me, and what kind of forms will I have to fill out?

Although the forms will vary somewhat from firm to firm, you should expect to supply such basic information as name, address, telephone number, occupation, and marital status. You probably also will be required to give a bank reference. You will need to sign a signature card so that the firm has a specimen of your signature to compare with documents that it receives in the future. Finally, and most important, you should expect to be asked to sign a detailed contract that covers the business relationship between you and the firm.

The broker needs to ask you detailed questions about your financial situation and your investment objectives. Good brokers try hard at this point to understand just what kind of investor you want to be. It is very important that the broker understand the level of risk you wish to take and how active an investor you wish to be. Some people put money into the stock market purely as a gamble, and they tend to enjoy the day-to-day playing of the game. Others are just the opposite, and merely wish to buy "safe" securities to put away for their retirement.

The most skillful brokers are able to learn more about your true desires than you even know yourself.

If by the time you are ready to sign the forms that open the account, you and the broker have not had a full discussion of your financial situation and investment objectives, I'd suggest you forget going ahead with that broker and instead begin searching for another one.

What are some of the specific things the broker should inquire about?

The broker needs to know a number of things relating to your financial situation and sophistication. For example, he or she may want to know:

- your annual income;
- your net worth;
- whether you have studied areas like business, finance, or accounting or know the basics of business from any other source, such as personal experience;
- whether you are or have been an officer, director, or substantial shareholder of any publicly held business, because that can affect your ability to sell securities of that company freely; and
- your experience in investing, including what kinds of securities you have bought in the past.

Single and Joint Accounts

I'm married; should an account be in both my and my spouse's names?

I can't answer that question for all situations, but I can give you some things to think about. First, if you put the account only in your name, anything in the account when you die will pass to your heirs either under the terms of your will or in accordance with what your state's law provides for people without wills. In this respect, the question of single or joint name needs to be answered as part of your estate plan. (I cannot go into detail about estate planning in this book; you might want to consult *Estate Planning: How to Preserve Your Estate for Your Loved Ones* by Jerome A. Manning, which is also published by the Practising Law Institute and is sold in bookstores.)

Is estate planning the only thing to take into account in deciding between a single or a joint account?

While estate planning is typically an important consideration, many people also have to consider how a brokerage account would affect the vulnerability of the family's assets in the case of a lawsuit against one or the other of the spouses. For example, the job of one spouse might subject him or her to a real risk of a judgment not covered by insurance. If you are concerned about the vulnerability of family assets to a judgment, you should discuss the brokerage account issue (and such related issues as who should hold title to the family house) with a lawyer who understands both the family's situation and the risk of a lawsuit that may not be satisfied by insurance.

Sometimes one spouse either brings substantial funds to a marriage or inherits such funds during the marriage. That spouse often wishes to keep those funds separate from family property. In that case, of course, that spouse probably would want to put such funds into an individual rather than a joint account.

What choices do I have if I do decide to set up a joint account?

Typically there are two options in setting up joint accounts, although that can vary by state, and the brokerage firm probably can be trusted to have its forms for establishing joint accounts take account of relevant state laws. The two typical ways in which people can share ownership of an account are as joint tenants (often phrased as joint tenants with right of survivorship) and as tenants in common.

In an account owned by joint tenants, the survivor takes ownership to the whole account automatically upon the death of the other joint tenant. When an account is owned by tenants in common, however, and when one joint account owner dies, his or her ownership in the account passes to his or her heirs under the terms of a will or state law. It does not automatically pass to the survivor. Spouses usually want to own an account as joint tenants, whereas business colleagues who pool their money to open an account typically want to be tenants in common. Make sure you know which kind of joint ownership you want, and make sure the forms you sign have the right choices indicated. (Note that sometimes you see joint tenancy with right of survivorship abbreviated as JTWROS or JTROS.)

Are there estate tax consequences from having a joint account?

Yes, there are. If married people are the joint owners, no federal estate tax has to be paid on an estate that passes to a spouse who is a U.S. citizen, no matter how large the estate. When, however, the account, or part of it, will pass to someone other than such a spouse, whatever portion of the account is considered by the tax laws to be in the deceased person's estate at the time of his or her death will be subject to estate tax. You can get into real messes here. Among other things, good records of contributions to the account, and anything else that may be relevant, are essential.

What are some of the specific estate tax considerations to be taken into account by spouses in determining what kind of account should be opened?

While no federal estate tax need be paid on an estate that passes to a spouse who is a U.S. citizen, there is at least one important federal tax consequence of having a spouse inherit an entire estate. The so-called unified credit for gift and estate taxes lets one leave, outright or in trust, up to $600,000 to children or others free from estate tax (assuming no gift tax liability). If the first spouse to die doesn't take advantage of this possibility, and, for example, leave money to his or her children, that spouse's $600,000 tax-free pass-on is lost forever.

Sometimes, of course, a substantial portion of a family's assets, besides the family house and personal property, is in a brokerage account. If an estate is large enough that the surviving spouse can maintain his or her lifestyle without inheriting all rights to the investment portfolio, it may be wise to have children or other heirs inherit, outright or in trust, some or all of the $600,000 that usually can be passed free from federal estate tax. (Under the proper kind of trust, income from the funds put in trust could go to the surviving spouse for his or her life and then the funds themselves could go to the children.) If anything like that is to be done, it needs to be part of an estate plan worked up by your lawyer, who can tell you what arrangements for an account or accounts he or she suggests with a brokerage firm. The estate plan for a large estate might, for example, contemplate two joint accounts, one held as joint tenants and the other held as tenants in common.

What about the gift tax consequences of joint and single accounts?

An investor needs to consider the federal and state gift tax consequences (a) of holding an account in joint name if the funds to be contributed are unequal (assuming equal ownership) or (b) of putting his or her funds in a single account owned by another person. In those kinds of situations, an investor would be wise to talk ahead of time to a lawyer who is expert in federal and state gift tax. (The general rule is that gifts to U.S. spouses are not taxable under federal law.)

Custodial and Special Accounts

What if I want to make a gift to one of my minor children or grandchildren, and I want to have that gift invested in securities. How do I handle that?

All or virtually all states have adopted either the Uniform Gifts to Minors Act or the Uniform Transfers to Minors Act. Under those laws, what you can do is open an account in your name as custodian for the child. The brokerage firm will have the forms to do that, and the mechanism is very simple. You will have the right to manage the account for the child. There are, of course, federal and state gift tax consequences to such a gift just as there are with any gift.

Here it is important to know that under current federal tax law there is an annual exemption from both the reporting requirement and the gift tax for gifts (other than gifts of future interests in property) totaling no more than $10,000 to each recipient. A married person sometimes can give up to $20,000 to each recipient, essentially using his or her spouse's exemption (consult your tax adviser about the ways and means of doing that).

Are single accounts, joint accounts, and accounts in the name of custodians for minors the only kinds of accounts I can open at a brokerage firm?

No, in appropriate circumstances you can open an account in the name of a corporation, a trust, a partnership, or some other entity or aggregate of people. You also can open special individual retirement accounts and accounts for other kinds of pension funds.

Discretionary Accounts

What is a discretionary account?

A discretionary account is an account that allows a broker to make buy-and-sell decisions for a customer on his or her own. The account may be in either a single account or a joint account. One of the forms you're asked to fill out may have a place for you to designate the account a discretionary account. Some brokerage firms, however, either do not allow discretionary accounts or allow only certain experienced and especially trusted brokers to administer discretionary accounts.

Should I consider a discretionary account?

Almost always, no. Brokers are paid commissions on trades, and no matter how honest the broker may be, a discretionary account gives a broker a serious conflict of interest. Beyond that, almost all brokers are essentially out to sell stock, and cannot be expected to make the best investment decisions. Typically, if an investor wants professional management, the way to get it is through either a mutual fund or an investment adviser, perhaps one who works for or through the brokerage firm the investor deals with. Some brokers, of course, are highly gifted money managers who do great jobs of managing discretionary accounts. A broker you deal with may possibly be in that category, but be 100 percent sure that's the case before entering into a discretionary account agreement. Among other things, I would suggest that you look for a long, consistent track record, including periods when the market was going down rather than up. Anybody can make money in a bull market.

Margin Accounts

Say I want to open a margin account; what more will be involved beyond what is necessary to set up a cash account?

Since a margin account will allow you to borrow a portion of the money needed to pay for securities, you will have to give information and sign documents relating to your situation as a borrower. You probably will not, however, find the requirements for setting up a margin account to be very tough.

Besides answering questions and filling out forms, are there any other requirements for establishing a margin account?

Yes, you will have to deposit a certain amount of money in cash, or a certain value of securities you already own, to open a margin account. The amount will vary from time to time and from firm to firm. The minimum is set by regulation, which can be changed at any time, and brokerage firms can require amounts in excess of the minimum. Two thousand dollars is the current minimum set by regulation.

If I have a margin account, what percentage of a security's price will I have to pay myself, and what percentage will I be able to borrow?

Under the Securities Exchange Act of 1934, the Federal Reserve Board has power to set the percentage of borrowed money that can be used to purchase or carry securities. The Board has adopted a number of regulations that set the so-called margin requirement in existence from time to time. Regulation T is the regulation that governs loans from brokerage firms. (Other regulations cover other borrowing situations, so don't try to avoid the margin requirements by borrowing money, for the purpose of purchasing or carrying securities, from a source other than a brokerage firm.) Currently the Federal Reserve Board allows a margin account investor to borrow from the brokerage firm up to 50 percent of the cost of stocks purchased for the account.

Why does the government get involved in telling me how much I can borrow to purchase stocks?

In the 1920s, there was no government regulation of borrowing to purchase stocks, and brokerage firms allowed customers to borrow almost all of the cost of securities they purchased. That worked quite well as long as the stock market continued to go up, but once it started to go down brokers were forced to sell their customers' securities in order to prevent the value of the securities from falling below the amount of the loans. All that selling drove the market lower and lower, and it helped to cause the stock market crash of 1929. It is in no one's interest to repeat that experience, and the Federal Reserve Board's regulations are designed specifically to prevent it.

What should I consider in deciding whether to open a margin account?

The first thing you have to consider is how much risk you are willing to take. Investing in the stock market is risky to start with, and buying on margin significantly increases that risk. It also, of course, increases the profit you can make if the stocks you purchase go up in value.

How does buying on margin increase both my risk and the amount of profit I can make?

Buying on margin increases your leverage, and that can work either for you or against you. The term "leverage" comes from the principal of the lever, of which a child's teeter-totter is a good example. If the teeter-totter is balanced on its midpoint, each end will go up and down the same amount. If you move the teeter-totter one way or the other, however, the long part will go up and down a much greater distance than will the short end. That is the principal of leverage, and it works in a similar way when you borrow money for an investment.

Take an example of buying a house. A home buyer may put down 10 percent and borrow 90 percent. Say the house costs $100,000. If the value of the house goes up to $110,000, the total increase in value will only be 10 percent, but the homeowner will have earned 100 percent on his or her $10,000 down payment. If, however, the house goes down in value to $90,000, the homeowner will have lost all of his or her down payment. The same thing happens when one buys stock on margin, except that in the case of a house the homeowner gets the value of being able to use the house, and except that the housing market is much less likely to drop as quickly or as much as the stock market. Note also that in my example I have not considered the interest that has to be paid on the borrowed money. In the case of a house, you can consider the interest as the equivalent of rent, and that's one of the reasons it makes more sense to use borrowed money to buy a house than it does to buy stock.

Remember, even if you guess right that a stock will go up in value, it has to go up enough to pay the brokerage commission on both the purchase and the sale of the stock, along with the interest paid on the money borrowed in the margin account, before you will make any personal profit. As an example, an investor could purchase a stock at $100 per share, and sell it several months later at $110 a share, and yet make no profit because of brokerage fees and interest. Buying on margin is usually not the smart thing for a new or unsophisticated investor to become involved in.

CLIENT AGREEMENT

What is a client agreement?

A client agreement is the (variously titled) document a brokerage firm often will have new clients sign at the time they set up an account. It is long, detailed, and filled with fine print.

How to Approach the Client Agreement

How should I approach the client agreement?

The best thing to do, of course, would be to read the client agreement very carefully before signing and to ask someone, perhaps a lawyer, to explain any parts of the agreement you do not fully understand. Very few people operate that way, however, and most people will sign the agreement after giving it only a short look. **That is a mistake.** There are one or two provisions in the agreement that I like to see crossed out before signing, and the investor should look for those provisions. We'll talk about those below.

Most of the agreement will turn out to be no problem and, after taking care of one or two important items, you can without too much worry sign the agreement without studying it carefully, on one condition. That condition is that you read the agreement carefully after getting it home. At that point if you find something that causes a problem, you can get it taken care of before going any further with the brokerage firm. It will cause no major problem if the agreement has to be redone. Also, if at that point you decide that you do not want to be a client of that brokerage firm, you can simply find a new firm to enter into an agreement with. The agreement you signed will not obligate you to continue the relationship.

What should I look for when I read the client agreement?

In general, you should read the agreement with two ideas in mind. First, you should look for provisions that you can't live with. Second, you should read the agreement to understand what the deal is going to be between you and the brokerage firm. Often, a client agreement is filled with information about how the brokerage firm operates. For example, sometimes there will be a provision that explains the terminology and procedures relating to the giving of buy-and-sell orders and the execution of those orders by the firm, along with information about the delivery of securities or cash as a result of those orders. It is very important that the investor know how all those things are done.

What law will govern the client agreement?

There almost certainly will be a provision in the agreement that specifies that a certain state's law will govern the agreement. Usually that state is New York, largely because so many brokerage firms are headquartered there. Almost all contracts of any type specify which state's law will govern, because it can be a real mess figuring that out after the fact if the parties don't choose a state. Basically, the law of any state that is somehow connected with the agreement, perhaps because one of the parties resides there or because the agreement was executed there, can be chosen. Although the law of New York on some point may be less favorable to an investor than the law of some other state, it is also true that New York's law may be more favorable to the investor on another point. One thing that is true is that New York is much more likely than any other state to have law on a specified question relating to a client agreement, because New York is the center of the securities industry.

How to Modify the Client Agreement

Are there clauses that I should cross out in the client agreement?

Yes, at least in some circumstances. For example, I discussed why you and a co-owner of the account might want to be tenants in common rather than joint tenants with right of survivorship (JTWROS). The client agreement may require you to cross out a provision presuming multiple owners of the account are JTWROS to achieve that result. In most cases, that clause is fine, because most joint accounts are owned by spouses and most times they want to be JTWROS. That clause could be absolutely disastrous, however, in a situation where the joint owners wanted to be tenants in common, so that upon the death of either of them that person's share in the account would pass to his or her heirs rather than to the other account owner. If you are opening a joint account, look at the agreement very carefully to see what it says on this point.

In addition, you may find any number of provisions that are a problem for you, and the agreement should be looked at with that in mind. A clause you may find is one requiring that disagreements be settled by arbitration rather than by a lawsuit, and I believe that clause should be crossed out.

What's wrong with arbitration? Isn't it quicker and cheaper than a lawsuit?

There is nothing necessarily wrong with arbitration, and it is typically quicker and cheaper than a lawsuit. That does not mean, however, that it is wise for you to roll over and play dead as to arbitration at the beginning of your dealings with the securities firm. Since securities firms hate lawsuits, your position likely will be much stronger in the case of a dispute if you have retained the right to bring one. Should a dispute arise, you can then decide to accept arbitration, with its advantages; it is highly unlikely that the brokerage firm will refuse.

How should I handle crossing out the arbitration clause?

I suggest you simply cross it out and hope the brokerage firm accepts the client agreement in that form. Nothing is likely to be gained by getting into a discussion with whomever you are dealing with about your feelings on arbitration. That person, usually the broker, wants your account and probably does not care about the arbitration clause. It is reasonable to hope, therefore, that the broker will not fight you on the point, but rather will just send the form up the line. However, simply crossing out the clause may or may not work. If the form is kicked back, I suggest you tell whomever you are dealing with that you do not believe it is fair at this point for you to have to commit yourself to arbitration.

What if the brokerage firm refuses to accept a contract with the arbitration clause crossed out?

The answer to that question depends on how happy you are in general with your choice of broker and brokerage firm and whether comparable firms are any more flexible on the issue. If you feel you have chosen the broker and firm you really want, or if you would have to use a firm with which you feel uncomfortable to avoid the clause, it probably makes sense to accept the arbitration clause in those circumstances. After all, only a very small percentage of investors ever find themselves facing arbitration or a lawsuit against their brokerage firm. Depending on how the firm handled your discussion of the client agreement, you may be questioning your choice of brokerage firm. In that case it may make sense to look for another firm.

Is there anything else I can do with the arbitration clause other than cross it out?

Another approach that might work, and that is probably more likely to be accepted than crossing out the clause, is to modify the clause to render it largely inapplicable. You could write in something like "Except for negligence or intentional wrongdoing" on the client agreement in a location that shows your intention that the words relate to the entire clause and not just to some part of it. Most things you would have disputes about would be caused by either negligence or intentional wrongdoing, and so modifying the agreement with the addition of the words I have suggested may end up having much the same effect as crossing through the clause. Handling the clause by adding words is not so sure as crossing out the clause, because you might later have to fight over what the words mean in the context and over the effect of the addition, but they still should at least give you very good leverage if a dispute that could lead to a lawsuit ever arises.

TITLE TO SECURITIES IN YOUR ACCOUNT

"Street Name"

When I buy securities through my account, will the certificates for the securities be put in my name?

One of the forms you fill out when opening your account should cover the question of how you will own the securities purchased for your account. Unless you specify otherwise in one of the forms, you probably will find that any securities you buy will be taken in what is called "Street name," and that will be required if you have a margin account. Taking securities in "Street name" means that the securities will not have your name on them as the owner, but rather they will have the name of the brokerage firm or some other entity on the books of the corporation that issued the securities.

For a great many securities, the usual choice of brokerage firms is to have the securities held in the name of Cede & Co., which is the so-called nominee of the Depository Trust Company, which is a company that holds title to securities for brokers and others in the securities industry. At the end of every trading day, the computers of the various securities firms figure out how many shares were bought and sold for their customers, and the books of the firms are changed to reflect the purchases and sales, as are the books of the Depository Trust Company. By this mechanism, the certificates for securities do not have to be exchanged for new ones every time the securities are sold. That is a big saving in trouble and money, and it is much safer to have the certificates kept in the vault of the Depository Trust Company rather than to have them sent back and forth to have names changed.

What if the Depository Trust Company, or some other such company, doesn't hold title to securities? Can they still be held in "Street name"?

Yes, a great many securities are simply kept in the name of some brokerage firm, even though neither that firm nor any of its customers any longer owns the securities. What happens is that brokerage firms simply transfer physical possession of the certificates representing the securities when the securities are sold by a customer, along with a power of attorney authorizing the change of record ownership. Firms typically keep securities in "Street name" because it is much easier than having names changed every time the securities change hands.

Record Title

What do the terms "record owner" and "beneficial owner" mean?

The record owner of a security is the owner shown on the books of the company that issued the security. The beneficial owner is the real owner of the security. He or she is the person who is shown on the books of a brokerage firm as owning them.

What if I want to have the securities put in my name when I buy them?

You have every right to do that, and in the forms you fill out to open an account some mechanism should be provided for you to do so. If you do decide to take record title in your own name, you should also be able to arrange for the brokerage firm to have the certificates either sent directly to you or safeguarded for you at the firm.

What are some of the advantages and disadvantages of taking record title to securities in your own name?

Holding record title makes it easier, as a practical matter, to move your account to a new brokerage firm. Unless you hold record title, you probably will not be able to participate in a corporation's dividend-reinvestment plan. Also, if you have record title to securities, and if you have physical possession of the certificates, you don't have to worry that the securities may be tied up for some period if your brokerage firm is closed because of bankruptcy. If you have record title to securities, but your brokerage firm has kept the certificates, you may find that they are unavailable to you for a short time if the firm goes bankrupt. You should be able, however, to get possession of the certificates fairly quickly. If you are not the record owner of securities and your brokerage firm goes bankrupt, your account (if it is your only one) generally will be insured by the Securities Investor Protection Corporation, which is a nonprofit corporation chartered by Congress, for up to $500,000 (of which up to $100,000 may be in cash). In addition, your brokerage firm may carry additional insurance on your account from a regular insurance company. Note that, insurance notwithstanding, it may take at least some weeks for you to have access to your securities or receive cash if your brokerage firm enters bankruptcy.

Because of the problems I may have if a brokerage firm goes bankrupt and I do not have record title to my securities, should I take title to my securities as record owner?

Generally, unless the amount in your account, or accounts if you have more than one, is in excess of the amount that is insured, I think the problems involved in holding title to securities outweigh the advantages you would have in the event of a firm's bankruptcy. As a matter of doing business, it is much easier not to have record title to your securities, and it is safer, too. If you do have record title, and especially if you have physical possession of certificates, you will have to go through a hassle every time you want to sell securities. After putting in an order to sell stock, you will have to get the stock certificate into the hands of your broker. To do that safely you either have to hand deliver it or send it by registered mail. At the same time you will need to get into your broker's hands what is called a stock power, and that stock power has to be signed by you and either hand delivered or mailed separately from the stock certificate. The stock power will be sent forward by your brokerage firm along with your stock certificate, and it is the stock power that authorizes the transfer of the certificate out of your name. (All this, along with the big problems and expenses you can encounter if certificates are lost, destroyed, or stolen, are discussed further in chapter 7.)

Note also that if the certificate you deliver is for more shares than you are selling, you will have to remember to check the mail over the coming weeks to see that you get a new certificate showing the shares that you still own, and you will have to put that certificate into safekeeping. If you hold record title to securities but have your brokerage firm keep the certificates in its vault, most of these problems are, of course, minimized.

Part II

MAKING
INVESTMENTS

Once you have a broker and a financial plan, you're ready to start making investments. In this part of the book we'll look at various types of investments in securities, and discuss the mechanics of investing. Included in this discussion will be questions and answers about the kinds of buy-and-sell orders that may be given to brokers, and about selling short and buying on margin. There is a chapter on dealing with your broker, and also one on buying securities directly from the companies that issue them, either in registered public offerings or in private placements and other so-called exempt offerings. Let's start by looking at questions relating to the simplest kind of investments to make, and then move to the more complex.

In reading chapter 4, I would suggest you keep in mind chapter 2: the questions discussed here are questions you would want to be sure your investment adviser has considered.

Insurance, Certificates of Deposit, and Mutual Funds

INSURANCE

Is life insurance an investment vehicle?

There are basically two types of life insurance. The first is term insurance. With term insurance, the money you spend goes only to provide insurance coverage, and the policy, therefore, never builds up any cash value. Term insurance is not an investment vehicle.

There are also many other kinds of life insurance that have two components. One component is term insurance. The other component is an extra amount that can be considered an investment, because the insurance company invests it for the policy holder to build up cash value. (I'll be calling this second type of insurance nonterm insurance.) The most traditional nonterm policies are whole life policies. With them you typically pay the same premium every year. In the early years, when you are younger, only some of your premium goes to pay for current insurance, while the rest of the amount you pay is invested by the insurance company. Later in your life, when the cost of current insurance is higher than your premium cost, the insurance company uses a portion of the fund you have built up to pay for current insurance.

What is your idea about term insurance versus nonterm insurance?

For some people, investing in nonterm life insurance makes sense. It is a conservative investment, and your money clearly is in the hands of professionals who usually can be trusted to do a reasonable job of management. Remember, however, that nonterm life insurance will require you at least to make set payments every year whether you are then in a good position to invest extra money in insurance or not (although borrowing against any built-up cash value in a nonterm policy to make premium payments usually is possible). (There are also some hybrid policies that require only a few, very large payments.) One big problem with nonterm life insurance, I believe, is that most people cannot afford to buy the amount of coverage they really need.

And so you favor term insurance?

For most people, I do believe term insurance is best. I also believe that, before making any decisions on the amount of money you have to invest, you should look carefully at your life insurance needs.

How much life insurance is enough?

The amount of life insurance one needs varies by situation. A young, single adult with no family responsibilities, or even a young couple with two good incomes and no children, may not need any life insurance. However, as a family comes more and more to depend on a person's income, that person's need for life insurance obviously increases. That need probably becomes greatest in the not uncommon situation of the wage-earner with a spouse and children who can be expected to need substantial income for the foreseeable future. A figure of six times annual earnings is sometimes suggested.

How sensible a multiple is six times earnings?

If you want your family to maintain its lifestyle for several decades, you have to think of more life insurance than six times earnings. Even ten times earnings wouldn't be enough by itself. Look at it this way. If someone has an annual income of $40,000, life insurance of ten times earnings would equal $400,000. Carefully invested, that amount could not be expected to yield anything like $40,000 in the first year, especially if something is set aside to allow for inflation. (If the proceeds of the insurance yield an income equaling only the amount the surviving family needs to live on in the first year, without any addition to principal to account for inflation, the amount of insurance clearly will be inadequate to do that in future years because of expected inflation.)

If, of course, you can plan that your family will need cash only for a set number of years, such as ten or fifteen, then you can calculate an amount of insurance that will be sufficient for the family's needs if they spend not only the income, but a part of the principal, every year. Before deciding that that amount of insurance is enough, remember that funds will not be put aside for your spouse's retirement, as you would be doing through a pension plan if you were alive. (On the other hand, if you have built up significant cash value in a pension fund that would be available immediately to your family on your death, that would decrease the amount of insurance you would have to carry.) Remember that most people at least hope that their income will go up every year in an amount equal to more than inflation. If you buy a policy that would allow the continuation of your family's lifestyle at the time of purchase, in a few years you may find that you have only half the insurance necessary to maintain your family's then current lifestyle. Here's a further thought to consider: it's smart to buy insurance when you know you can pass the medical exam. If you wait until you feel you really need the insurance, you may not be able to buy it. (Also, don't forget about disability insurance; it's as important as life insurance, and sometimes more important.)

How do I find the best deals on life insurance?

You really have to look carefully, because the cost of insurance varies a great deal. Most of the major companies are more interested in selling you nonterm insurance than term insurance, and so you may have to do a bit of searching to find a good deal on term insurance. You want either a company that sells direct with no commissions to salespersons or a company that sells with minimal commissions. One suggestion is to go to your library and look for articles in reputable magazines that evaluate the term insurance offered by various life insurance companies. (The *Reader's Guide to Periodical Literature* and computer databases should be helpful.)

If I do have life insurance with a cash value, should I borrow against the cash value to get money for investing?

It is unlikely that you should. While you often can borrow against life insurance at a favorable interest rate, any investment you make still has to be good enough not only to earn you a return in the ordinary sense, but good enough also to cover the interest on the loan. If you can consistently find investments like that, you don't need a book on investor's rights, you need a book on yacht repair. Note also that the Federal Reserve Board's margin requirements apply to loans taken for purchasing or carrying securities.

CERTIFICATES OF DEPOSIT

What is a certificate of deposit?

A certificate of deposit is a certificate indicating that a given amount of money has been deposited at the bank that issued the certificate. The certificate will specify the number of days the money is to be on deposit and the interest rate to be paid. Since they generally are insured, certificates of deposits usually are very safe investments. Even the most sophisticated investors often put their money in CDs for short periods while they are waiting for a better investment to come along.

Can I invest in certificates of deposit only through banks?

No, brokerage firms very often can put you into certificates of deposit from banks around the country. It's smart to check with your broker if you are interested in investing in a CD, because the interest rate available from a bank in some other city may be better than you can get at a local bank.

Will I have to pay a brokerage commission if I invest in CDs through a brokerage firm?

Usually you will not have to pay a brokerage fee for a CD. In most cases the brokerage firm gets its commission from the bank that issued the CD.

MUTUAL FUNDS

What are mutual funds?

Mutual funds are companies that take in money from investors and then invest that money in stocks, bonds, or other securities. By owning a mutual fund share, what the individual investor really owns, indirectly, is a small piece of all the securities that the mutual fund owns. Another term for a mutual fund is "investment company." Mutual funds are heavily regulated by the Securities and Exchange Commission under the Investment Company Act of 1940.

Types of Mutual Funds Available

What are the types of mutual funds available?

There are two basic ways to categorize mutual funds:

1. as load, low-load, or no-load funds; and
2. as open-end or closed-end funds.

What is the difference between load, low-load, and no-load funds?

Low-load funds involve, as a "front-end load," a sales commission of up to 3 percent when you purchase them. Load funds have a front-end load of between 3 percent and 8.5 percent. Obviously, no-load funds carry no sales commission. Funds with a front-end load of 3 percent or over are sold through brokerage firms and some investment advisers, financial planners, and insurance agents, whereas low-load and no-load funds are almost always sold directly by the mutual funds themselves.

In evaluating the relative costs of investing in the various types of mutual funds, be sure to consider charges other than front-end loads. Many low-load and no-load funds have a back-end load. These back-end loads, which can run to several percent, are charges made at the time shares are sold. In addition, many funds charge a so-called 12b-1 fee of up to 1.25 percent. That fee, which gets its name from the rule of the Securities and Exchange Commission that allows it, is basically to pay promotional expenses. Typically, the brokerage firm that put the investor into the mutual fund is paid all or part of this fee by the mutual fund every year the investor stays in the fund.

All funds have an annual charge for expenses, of which a management fee is the largest component. These expenses generally run from about 0.5 percent to about 1.5 percent of the average value of all the securities in the fund during a particular period, but sometimes they run much higher. These expenses are not paid out of investors' pockets, but rather the mutual fund takes them out of the funds it has under management. Obviously, you are better off, other things being equal, putting your money into a fund that has only a charge for expenses — and the lower the expenses the better.

What is the difference between open-end funds and closed-end funds?

Closed-end funds register with the Securities and Exchange Commission only a specified number of shares that they wish to sell to the public. When those shares have been sold, the fund is considered closed, and, after that time, the only way you can buy shares in the fund is to buy them in the trading markets, just the way you buy shares of stock. An open-end fund, conversely, has no set number of shares that it will issue. Rather, it registers with the Securities and Exchange Commission, from time to time, whatever number of shares it believes it may be able to sell in the foreseeable future. In the case of open-end funds, then, the investor always can buy shares in the fund directly from the fund itself.

What kinds of securities do mutual funds invest in?

There is a vast multitude of mutual funds, and they cover the full spectrum of possibilities for investing in securities. For example, some invest in stocks, some in bonds, and some in a mix of stocks and bonds. Some invest in stocks of companies in a particular industry. Some invest only in European companies or Asian companies. Some own only the stocks in one of the indexes. Some mutual funds invest only in companies that follow certain specified ethical practices. One of the most helpful ways to categorize mutual funds by kinds of investment is to separate them by risk levels. If you're looking for really low-risk funds, there are many that invest only in the safest kinds of bonds. At the other end of the spectrum, it is possible to find mutual funds that invest in the companies they believe offer the greatest potential of profit irrespective of risk.

Should Mutual Funds Be Considered?

Should I consider investing in a mutual fund?

Before you decide to invest in securities on your own, you should consider mutual funds. With mutual funds, you get professional management and diversification of your investments. You need to decide if that is what you want. You need to decide if you really want to jump into investing on your own with both feet, if you're willing to devote the time necessary to making good investment decisions, and if you have the needed skills. Some investors take investing as a form of personal challenge, viewing it much as they would a chess game. Mutual funds may not give them what they want from investing. You must decide if you are one of those people. Certainly there is no set answer to whether individual investors should buy mutual fund shares or should pick securities on their own.

How to Choose a Mutual Fund

What should I consider in choosing a mutual fund?

One problem with investing in mutual funds is that picking a mutual fund can be as difficult as picking a good stock. With the large number of mutual funds to choose from, it may seem impossible for an investor to make a reasonable choice. I have some suggestions about choosing a mutual fund that should make the job manageable. First, of course, you must choose the risk level you want to buy into. Making that decision should be part of your financial plan. You must decide if you want to look for a fund with some special characteristic (such as one that buys stock of companies in a particular industry). You should, of course, consider the front- and back-end loads, and other charges, involved in various funds. Certainly, too, past performance is very important.

How can I find good mutual funds to invest in?

A recommendation from a trusted investment professional, such as a financial planner or your broker, is one way you might find good mutual funds to invest in, and your brokerage firm may have research reports available on mutual funds. When looking at such recommendations or reports, however, remember that, depending on the circumstances, the only funds that will be recommended or reported on may be funds with a front-end load. Financial magazines often carry reports and evaluations on various mutual funds, and a visit to your library (or perhaps a business school's library) and a search for a number of those articles is one starting point. Also, there are specialized publications the library may carry that report on the performance of mutual funds.

One smart thing to do is check the evaluations of funds, and the reports of their performances, over a number of years. Make sure you don't just look at the last years' performance, especially if the market has been generally up during the period. Even a fund managed by nitwits can do well for a year here or there. It will be especially helpful to check the performance of funds during periods when the market has been either down or erratic.

If I do decide to put my money in mutual funds, should I put it all in one fund?

One of the benefits of investing in a mutual fund is the diversity of investment that the fund provides. Considering all the various types of funds available, you probably can find a fund that fits your specifications and has had superior performance in the recent past. If, however, your research into mutual funds leads you to two or three funds that you believe together will best suit your desires, I see no reason why you shouldn't go with them.

Monitoring Performance

How carefully do I have to monitor the performance of a mutual fund I have invested in?

While you should not feel you have to check performance every week, you definitely should not simply put your money in a fund and forget about it. Even funds with the very best track records sometimes falter. In fact, that should be expected at some time during a fund's life, due, if for no other reason, to changes in fund managers over time. Do monitor the performance of your fund, and check it against that of other funds periodically, so that you can move your money when it makes sense to do so. As to how often one should evaluate a fund's performance, that is to a large extent a personal question. Some people enjoy looking after their investments on a more or less continual basis, while others invest in mutual funds partly because they cannot stand monitoring investments and want simply to turn money management over to the fund. My personal thought is that you should monitor a fund's performance at least every few months whether you feel like it or not, and you should monitor it otherwise whenever something comes to your attention to trigger a question in your mind about the fund's performance.

CHAPTER

5

Mechanics of Investing

COMMON TYPES OF SECURITIES

What is common stock?

Common stock is the basic ownership interest in a corporation. In most circumstances, the owners of a corporation's common stock are the ones who elect directors, vote on all changes to the corporation's charter, have a right to receive all dividends declared by the board of directors after any dividends on any preferred stock have been paid, and have a right to receive the corporation's assets, after creditors and holders of preferred shares have been paid, if the corporation is liquidated.

Some corporations have more than one class of common stock. When they do that they simply vary some of the rights of the owners of the various classes. For example, one class may have the right to vote for directors and the other class may not. Common stock is an equity security, in that it represents the interest of an owner in the corporation. This sets it apart from debt securities, such as bonds, that make the holder of the security a creditor of the corporation.

What is preferred stock?

Preferred stock is stock that is preferred over a corporation's common stock in some way or other. Typically, holders of preferred shares have a right to receive a certain amount of money per share if the corporation is dissolved, after debts have been paid, before the common shareholders receive anything. Usually also, preferred shareholders have a right to receive a certain specified dividend before the common shareholders receive a dividend. (Note that this does not mean that holders of preferred shares have a legal right to dividends. The board of directors has to declare dividends and announce them before anyone has a right to them.)

An important distinction here is that, almost always, the rights to dividends of holders of preferred shares will be limited to a specified amount. That means that those holders do not typically share in the corporation's successes beyond an agreed level. Any other dividends that are to be paid, no matter how great, will be paid to the common shareholders in the typical corporation. Preferred stock dividends usually are made cumulative, which means that no dividends may be paid to the common shareholders until all dividends that should have been paid on the preferred shares have been paid.

Typically, holders of preferred shares do not have a right to vote on most matters that are submitted for a shareholders' vote. If, however, preferred stock dividends are not paid for a stated period, often twelve months, many corporations give their holders of preferred shares the right to elect some or all of the corporation's directors until all dividends in arrears are paid.

Unlike typical common stock, preferred stock usually is callable. That is, the board of directors typically is able to force the holders of preferred shares out of the corporation upon the payment to them of an amount of cash that is specified in the corporation's charter. Technically, preferred stock is an equity security. It represents an ownership interest in the company as a legal matter. In practical terms, however, preferred stock usually seems more like a debt security, such as a bond.

Preferred stock may be of special interest to an investor if it is convertible into common stock (see below).

Stocks often are said to have a certain "par value"; what is par value?

Par value is a creation of state law, and is most simply seen as a dollar amount per share, which is stated in the corporation's founding document, from which certain consequences flow under state law:

1. The corporation cannot issue stock for less than par. Since a common value is $1, that's not a major restriction.
2. When stock is issued, at whatever price, the par value goes on the corporation's books as what is often called "stated capital." State corporation laws limit what can be done with amounts in stated capital; for example, no dividends may be paid out of it.

3. Fees and taxes payable to the state of incorporation often are based on par value. Stock without par value is convenient for a corporation in some respects, but often fees and taxes on stock without par value are calculated as if the stock's par value were $100. That is one reason having stock without par value is still not so common as having stock with a par value, typically a low one such as $1.

Although, as you can see, par value has little importance to investors in established stocks, the term is used in prospectuses and on stock certificates and investors should be aware of it.

Some stocks are said to be "convertible"; what does that mean?

"Convertible" means that a stock can under specified circumstances, at the option of the owner, be converted into another kind of stock. For example, the owner of a share of convertible preferred stock typically would have the right to convert that stock into common stock on a ratio, and under circumstances, that are spelled out in the corporation's charter. Not only can one kind of stock be convertible into another kind of stock, but debt securities, such as bonds or debentures, can be made convertible into preferred or common stock.

What kind of investors typically buy preferred stock?

Preferred stock is usually sold to institutions, such as savings banks and insurance companies, that have special reasons for wanting to own preferred stock. Very little preferred stock in publicly held companies is ever purchased by ordinary investors. Almost always they prefer common stock, because it typically has a much greater chance to increase in value than does preferred stock.

The partial exception to that statement, as I suggested above, is convertible preferred stock. If the ratio at which the stock can be exchanged is a generous one, then, under certain circumstances, preferred stock can be a way to capture appreciation in the underlying common stock while receiving a more secure dividend while you're waiting.

What does it mean when a stock is called a "blue chip" stock?

The term "blue chip" is a loose term used to describe stocks of stable, old-line companies that offer investors a relatively safe investment. Typically these companies pay dividends on their common stock and, because of the stability of the companies, those dividends are more secure than are the dividends of companies generally. The downside of owning blue chip stocks is that they aren't likely to increase dramatically in value.

What is a bond?

In terms of corporations, the term "bond" is usually used to describe a long-term debt instrument (often one that is not due to be paid for twenty or thirty years) that is secured by a mortgage or deed of trust on corporate property. Government bonds are long-term debt instruments that are much like corporate bonds, but government bonds typically are not secured by specific property.

Corporate bonds typically are issued under the terms of what is called an indenture, which is a contract between the corporation and a trustee, usually a bank, that acts for the benefit of the bond holders. For example, the indenture will contain provisions that require the corporation to do certain things (for example, maintaining certain accounting ratios) and to refrain from certain other things (for example, paying dividends above a certain amount). During the life of the bond, the trustee is given the job of monitoring the corporation's acts to see if it is in compliance with the terms of the indenture. If it is not, the trustee can take the corporation to court in an attempt to protect the interests of the bond holders.

What is a debenture?

In general financial parlance, a debenture is much like a corporate bond, except that debentures are not secured by any property, but rather by the general credit of the company. They are, however, typically issued under an indenture, just as bonds are. Debentures typically have shorter terms than do bonds. For example, if a corporation issues bonds payable in twenty-five or thirty years, any debentures it issues might be due in fifteen or twenty years.

What is a note?

In financial terms, a note is yet another type of debt instrument. Notes may be secured or unsecured, but they are almost never issued under indentures the way bonds and debentures are. Also, notes are generally for much shorter terms than are bonds or debentures.

What are options and warrants?

The terms "options" and "warrants" are synonymous. An option or a warrant is a right to purchase some other security of the corporation that granted the option or warrant. Typically, that other security is common stock. Under the usual option or warrant, the holder has the right to exercise the option or warrant for the purchase of a set number of shares of common stock at a specified price.

Most options and warrants have limited duration, so that after they expire they have no value. Under securities law, options and warrants are themselves securities, so that all the protections of the securities laws that exist for the protection of investors apply to options and warrants, just the way they do to stocks.

The value of an option or a warrant is related to the value of underlying common stock. Obviously, the right to buy a $50 share for $45 should be worth around $5. Options and warrants are sometimes used in takeovers and initial public offerings because they give value without costing the issuer anything at the time they are issued. Options and warrants can trade in the public markets just like any other securities.

What are puts, calls, and straddles?

A put is a contractual right to sell a specified amount of a given security at a particular price. A call is the contractual right to buy a given amount of a particular security at a specified price. A straddle is a contract that contains both a put and a call for the same security. Puts, calls, and straddles on securities of publicly held companies can be purchased from brokerage firms just the way stocks can.

As in the case of options and warrants, under the securities laws puts, calls, and straddles are themselves securities, so that people who invest in them have the same protections that the securities laws offer investors in stocks.

What are American depositary receipts?

American depositary receipts are receipts, issued by American banks, that evidence an indirect ownership interest in a foreign security that is owned (or at least controlled) by the bank. These receipts, which typically are simply called ADRs, often provide an investor with the simplest way to "own" securities issued by other than American or Canadian companies. The banks that issue ADRs iron out the problems an investor would have if he or she owned the foreign securities directly. For example, the bank will collect dividends paid in foreign currencies and convert them into dollars before paying them over to the owner of the ADRs. The complications that can be involved in the physical transfer of foreign securities owned by Americans are also avoided because it is only the ADR that changes hands from one investor to another in America, not the underlying foreign security. ADRs are themselves securities; investors can buy and sell them through brokerage firms.

STOCK EXCHANGES

What are stock exchanges?

Stock exchanges are organizations that provide a marketplace for buying and selling securities. Despite being called *stock* exchanges, many other kinds of securities, such as bonds and stock options, are traded there. A typical stock exchange will be made up of members who hold what are called seats. Note, the ads you may have seen on television for the exchange of the future refer to a computerized equivalent of the exchanges I am going to be discussing at this point; I'll get to NASDAQ shortly.

How do exchanges work?

Most broadly, each exchange provides a place (typically a large room, called the "floor") where members, or more usually employees of members, gather to buy and sell securities for themselves or their customers. In the case of the two largest exchanges, the New York Stock Exchange and the American Stock Exchange, the trading goes on in two separate buildings in the Wall Street area of New York City.

People working on the floor of the exchange get buy-and-sell orders from brokerage houses all over the country. Specific securities are traded at designated places on the floor called posts, and usually the members' representatives having buy or sell orders go to the proper post and execute their orders.

Essentially what happens is that the exchange conducts a continual auction of the various securities traded on that exchange. We'll talk later about how orders are given to and executed by brokerage firms.

How do companies arrange for their securities to trade on a stock exchange?

Each exchange has its own requirements for listing a particular security for sale on the exchange. The bigger and more prestigious the exchange, the more stringent those requirements are.

How do the exchanges differ?

The New York Stock Exchange is the largest and most prestigious, and therefore it has listing requirements that allow only the securities of the largest companies to be traded there. Next in line is the American Stock Exchange, on which trade the securities of small and medium-size companies. In addition to those two exchanges, there are a number of so-called regional exchanges around the country. They tend to trade the securities of small, often regional companies, plus they often also trade the securities of some of the companies that are listed on the New York or American Exchanges. Through a computer service called the Intermarket Trading System, brokers and others can compare the prices of trades for a given security on various exchanges.

Does the federal government regulate stock exchanges?

Yes, the Securities Exchange Act of 1934, which was passed in response to abuses in the securities industry that helped lead to the stock market crash of 1929 and the depression that followed, regulates stock exchanges. That law has provisions that regulate those exchanges directly, and it also gives the Securities and Exchange Commission broad powers to pass regulations governing the operation of "national" exchanges. (For purposes of federal law, the regional exchanges are considered "national" exchanges.) The Securities Exchange Act of 1934 also gives exchanges the power to regulate their own affairs, and for this reason exchanges are often referred to as self-regulatory organizations, or SROs. At the same time, the law gives the SEC the power to oversee the exchanges' self-regulation, including the power to approve or disapprove any rules an exchange wishes to pass for its own regulation.

OVER-THE-COUNTER MARKET

What is the over-the-counter market?

Unlike the situation with stock exchanges, there is no single place where securities are bought and sold in the over-the-counter market. The term "over-the-counter" refers to the way in which securities that are not listed on an exchange are sold through securities firms acting as dealers. The term comes from the fact that, in a sense, securities firms sell securities directly to investors in the same sort of way that stores sell merchandise "over the counter."

How does the over-the-counter market work?

In the case of each publicly held company whose securities are not traded on an exchange, securities firms decide whether they wish to do what is called "making a market" in that company's securities. Typically at least two or three securities firms will decide to do so, and sometimes the number is much greater. To make a market in a security, a securities firm simply maintains an inventory of that security. It then publishes two prices, which change sometimes on a minute-by-minute basis. Those prices are the bid price, which is the price the securities firm will pay for the security, and the ask price, which is the price the firm will sell the security for. An investor who wants to buy or sell an over-the-counter security usually goes to his or her broker. The broker checks the prices quoted by various market makers and then is supposed to do the transaction for the investor with the firm that offers the best price.

How do brokers check prices in the over-the-counter market?

For a large number of securities, a broker merely needs to call up on the broker's computer screen the prices offered by various market makers. This is done through a system known as the National Association of Securities Dealers Automated Quotation system, which is abbreviated NASDAQ. For the prices of less frequently traded securities, however, the broker must check what are called the "pink sheets," which are literately pink sheets of paper giving the latest bid and ask prices quoted by various market makers. The pink sheets, as might be expected, have quotations for the smallest publicly held corporations.

How is the over-the-counter market regulated?

The regulation of the over-the-counter market parallels to a great extent the regulation of stock exchanges. The Securities Exchange Act of 1934 regulates the activities of those involved in the over-the-counter market. That Act also gives the Securities and Exchange Commission the power to pass regulations concerning that market. In addition, the Act provides for the registration and regulation of what it calls "national securities associations." The only such association is the National Association of Securities Dealers, Inc. Like stock exchanges, the NASD is a self-regulatory organization. It has power to make its own rules governing the activities of its members, and the SEC has the power to oversee all the activities of the NASD, including the rules it makes. Almost all securities firms in the country are members of the NASD, and thus are subject to its rules.

BASICS OF BUYING AND SELLING SECURITIES

Buy-and-Sell Orders

How is a buy or sell order executed?

It depends on whether the trade is to be on a securities exchange or in the over-the-counter market. For securities trading on an exchange, your broker will, by one means or another, transmit your order to the trading floor at the exchange. The order sometimes will be passed to one of the firm's floor brokers, who will go to the place on the floor, called a "post," where the security you want to buy or sell is traded. In the case of relatively small orders, the order will usually be passed electronically to the post. At the post will be someone called a "specialist." Specialists essentially run auctions for the securities they handle, although they also buy and sell secu-

rities themselves if that is necessary to ensure that someone at the post is always willing to buy and always willing
to sell. Securities will be bought or sold for you in accordance with the terms of your order, and then word will
be sent to your broker that the order has been executed.

How are buy-and-sell orders handled differently in the over-the-counter market?

In the over-the-counter market, your broker or a clerk
will compare prices of the various firms that make a market in the securities you are interested in, and they are
supposed to buy from or sell to the market maker that offers the best deal.

What are the various options I have in placing orders to buy or sell securities?

There are many different types of orders. Some of the
common types that relate to the price at which you are
willing to buy or sell are the market order, stop order,
limit order, and stop-limit order. There are also a number of orders that cover the period of time you want the
order to be open for. Examples are the open — or
"good-until-cancelled" — order and the day order.

What is a market order?

A market order is an order to buy or sell "at the market."
This means that the order is to be put through at the best
price obtainable, during the normal trading session,
when the order hits the trading floor, in the case of exchange-traded securities, or when your brokerage firm
can accomplish the transaction, in the over-the-counter
market. Typically, before giving a market order, you have

your broker check the most recent prices reported, and, unless you're trading on an unusually volatile day, the price at which you purchase or sell should not be startlingly different from what you expect. In today's electronic environment, of course, you can determine many prices throughout the day by watching cable television or querying a computer database.

What is a limit order?

In a limit order, you give your broker the maximum price you will pay if you are buying or the minimum price you will take if you are selling. For example, if recent trades have been at around $45 per share and that is all you are willing to pay, you can put in a limit order to buy a set number of shares at $45. If your firm can buy at $45 or less it will do so. Otherwise your order will not be executed.

What is a stop order?

A stop order, sometimes called a stop-loss order, is an order to buy or sell a security, at the market price, when the security has traded at or beyond the price you specify. That price is called a "stop price." Stop orders are often used to limit losses or to lock in profits. A benefit of the stop order is that you can decide ahead of time at what price you want to buy or sell and, as long as the order remains in existence, you do not have a great need to fear that you will miss the chance to get in or out at approximately the price you want. I say "approximately" because, although a stop order is triggered at a particular price, there is no guarantee that your brokerage firm will be able to put through your trade at that same price.

What is a stop-limit order?

A stop-limit order combines aspects of the limit order and the stop order. It is an order to buy or sell, at a price that you set, once a trade has occurred at or beyond a certain price, which may or may not be the same as the purchase or sale price you have specified. If the securities cannot then be purchased or sold at the price you have set, or at a better price, the order will not be executed. Take, for example, the situation where you have purchased securities at $45 per share and they currently trade at $55 per share. Perhaps the market is going through a volatile period, and you would like to lock in a reasonable profit if you can, but you do not want to sell out too cheaply just because the market may take a quick, rebounding dip. You might put in a stop-limit order at $50 (stop) $49 (limit), figuring that if the market hits $50 you are willing to sell at a price at or above $49, but that you are not willing to sell if the market price dips even further. If you're right that any dip below $49 will be temporary, your stop-limit order will have saved you from selling out too cheaply. If, however, the market continues down, you may wish that you had simply put in a stop order at $50 and allowed the trade to go through at the best price obtainable at that point.

What is a good-until-cancelled order?

A good-until-cancelled order, also called an open order, stays in effect until you cancel it or until it is executed (although, as a practical matter, brokerage firms may set limits on how long they are willing to keep orders on their books).

What is a day order?

A day order expires at the end of the trading day if it hasn't been executed. Market orders are generally understood to be day orders.

Will my brokerage firm treat orders in the ways you have discussed?

You should find that the types of orders the firm will take are spelled out in some written document, commonly the client agreement discussed above. You definitely should check, by asking questions if necessary, for the details of how your brokerage firm treats various orders. Other types of orders, beyond those discussed above, will be available for you to use. Also, your brokerage firm's treatment of orders may differ from what is stated above.

Do I need to keep a record of orders?

Yes, you need to make your own written notes when you place orders, and those notes should include the date and time and all the particulars of the order.

Round and Odd Lots

Is there any advantage to trading shares in hundred-share units?

When buying on a stock exchange, yes. In the over-the-counter market, there at least generally is no such benefit. On at least the New York and American Stock Exchanges, stock trades in hundred-share lots, and so, if you trade either one hundred shares or a multiple of one hundred, you are trading in round lots. Any amount of fewer than one hundred shares is an odd lot, and you will have to pay what is called an odd-lot differential for each share you purchase in an odd lot. There is an exception to the rule that shares trade in lots of one hundred. For shares whose trading is inactive, you may find that the round lot is ten.

Why is there an odd-lot differential, and how much is it?

It costs more to trade in odd lots because the trading of odd lots is handled in a more cumbersome way on the floor of the exchange. Odd lots are sold through odd-lot dealers rather than through the usual auction mechanism. These dealers buy and sell shares for their own accounts. The odd-lot differential is quite small. Typically it has been one-eighth point or one-quarter point per share. One point is $1, so one-eighth point is 12.5 cents and one-quarter point is 25 cents per share. The effect of the odd-lot differential can vary with brokerage firms, because some adjust their commissions for small investors.

Do bonds also trade on exchanges in round lots?

Yes, though in a slightly different sense. Typical round lots for bonds are face values of $1,000 and $100,000.

Margin Account Trading

How do the mechanics of buying securities differ if I have a margin account?

As discussed in chapter 3, a margin account allows you to borrow from the brokerage firm a certain percentage of the purchase price of most stocks. Currently, that amount is set by the Federal Reserve Board's regulation T at 50 percent. Just because you have a margin account, however, you do not have to use the credit available to you. You can use your own money to cover the entire purchase price of stocks if you wish.

Are the mechanics of selling securities any different in a margin account?

The mechanics of selling securities can be different if you have a margin account, in one respect. In a margin account, any securities you own must be held in "Street name." If you merely had a cash account and chose to hold title to securities in your own name and take physical possession of the certificates, you would have to deliver those certificates when you sell the securities. As discussed earlier, holding securities in "Street name" greatly simplifies the mechanics of delivering securities when you sell them.

Why do securities have to be held in "Street name" in a margin account?

When you have a margin account, the securities you purchase are held by the brokerage firm as security for money lent to you. If the brokerage firm has to sell those securities to protect its loan, it wants to be able to do so without the problems it would have if those securities were in your name and, especially, if you had physical possession of the certificates.

What interest do I have to pay on margin loans from a brokerage firm?

The interest rate varies greatly from time to time and, to some extent, from brokerage house to brokerage house.

The rates are favorable, however, with a typical rate being not too much above the prime rate (the rate charged by banks to their best customers). The relatively low interest rate is due to at least three factors. First, the loan is secured by stock that is in the possession of the brokerage firm. Second, the loan is for only up to 50 percent of the purchase price of securities, giving the brokerage firm a comfortable cushion in terms of collateral for the loan. Third, margin account loans are, under the contract you signed with the brokerage firm, payable on demand at any time the brokerage firm wants to call them. This gives the brokerage firm extra protection, since it can get out of the loan if, for some reason, it feels insecure.

Where do brokerage firms get the money to lend on margin accounts?

They may use some of their money, but typically all or part of the money used for margin loans comes from banks. To secure those loans the brokerage firms usually pledge your securities to the bank as collateral. Typically, then, the brokerage firm makes a profit by charging you an interest rate slightly higher than the firm itself obtains from the bank.

What happens if I buy a stock on margin and the stock goes down in value?

If the stock goes down very much, you will receive what is known as a "margin call." Under the so-called maintenance requirements of the stock exchanges and the National Association of Securities Dealers, Inc., you must at all times have equity in a margin account that is equal to at least a set percentage, typically 25 percent, of the then current market value of the stocks in the account. Brokerage firms can require that you maintain an even higher equity in your margin account, and most do. Something on the order of 35 percent equity should be expected. By "equity" I mean the value of the stocks in your account minus the amount of the margin loan. (Note that the maintenance requirement is somewhat higher if you have sold stocks short, something that is discussed below.)

What happens if my equity falls below the figure allowed by my brokerage firm and I get a margin call?

You will be notified by the firm that the market value of your stocks has fallen to the point that you need to deposit more money, or nonmargined securities, to increase your equity to the required amount. Under your contract with your brokerage firm, the firm undoubtedly will have power to demand immediate payment and, failing that, it can begin selling securities from your account to protect the security of the loan. That drastic an action is unlikely, however, and typically you will be given a short amount of time, perhaps one or two days, to deposit whatever amount is necessary to bring your equity up to the level your brokerage firm requires.

Can all stocks be bought on margin?

Almost all stocks that would interest a typical investor can be bought on margin. Stocks that are listed on stock exchanges, over-the-counter stocks that are part of NASDAQ's National Market System, and some over-the-counter stocks that are not part of the National Market System can be bought on margin. In general, only the stock of small, relatively obscure companies may not be purchased on margin. Your broker should be able to tell you promptly whether a particular stock can be bought on margin.

Is the interest I pay on a margin loan tax-deductible?

Sometimes interest on a margin loan is deductible and sometimes it is not. As is usual in the tax area, there are tricks, and you will need to check the tax rules carefully for details that vary greatly from one circumstance to another. You will find, for example, that margin interest is deductible only if it is less than or equal to what is called "net investment income." You will also find that interest on money used to buy or carry tax-exempt securities is not deductible. One of the real tricks there is determining what may be considered "carrying" securities. It is fair to say that you can have trouble with that concept in many circumstances when you borrow money at a time when you own tax-exempt securities.

Selling Short

What does it mean to sell short?

Selling short means you sell securities at a time when you either do not own those securities or, even though you own them, you are not able to, or do not wish to, sell the securities you own. The latter situation is known in the industry as selling short "against the box."

How do you accomplish a short sale?

You can sell short only if you have a margin account. If you have a margin account, selling short is essentially like any other sale. Under standard business practice for a sale of most securities, the seller needs to deliver a certificate for the securities sold within five business days. An order for a short sale is put through in the same way any other order is, but the difference is that instead of delivering your securities in five business days, you arrange through your brokerage firm to borrow the securities to be delivered.

From whom are the securities borrowed?

Your brokerage firm usually borrows the securities from one of its customers who has a margin account. Often margin customers consent to such arrangements in a standard clause in the firm's margin account agreement. Also, many brokerage firms have agreements with other firms that allow borrowing across firm lines. Once in a while a brokerage firm has to borrow securities from an institutional investor.

Am I charged for borrowing securities when I sell short?

You are not charged typically if the securities come from your brokerage firm or a firm with which your firm has a reciprocal arrangement. You will be charged, however, if the securities you borrow come from an institutional investor.

What are the financial arrangements I'll have to make in connection with a short sale?

The brokerage firm will hold the proceeds of the sale as security for the loan. In addition, you will have to have in your margin account, by the addition of cash or non-margined securities if necessary, an amount equal to 50 percent of the market value of the securities that you sold short. Typically, you will be given five business days to make any required deposit into the margin account. If the price of the securities you have sold short goes up, the maintenance rules of the stock exchanges and the NASD, along with the brokerage firm's own maintenance requirements, come into play. This works in essentially the same way I discussed above in connection with margin accounts generally. If there is, for example, a 30 percent maintenance requirement, you will find that the price of the securities you purchase can increase somewhat over 15 percent before you are required to deposit additional funds in order to bring your margin account into compliance with the 30 percent maintenance requirement.

How do I close out a short sale?

Typically, you will buy securities in the market to pay back the account you borrowed from. Obviously, if the market has risen since your short sale, you will lose money. What you hope is that the price of the securities will have gone down, so that you can buy them for less than you sold them for in your short sale.

I probably should point out that short selling differs from other securities transactions in that you could, in theory, be liable for an open-ended amount. If you own a security, the worst that can happen is that it will go to zero, and you will lose your investment and whatever you owe on your margin account. If you sell short, however, the price of the stock could go through the roof, and you would owe whatever it took to buy the shares to cover your short position. In one historic battle for control of a railroad early in this century, under less restrictive laws, some speculators sold short stock they were not sure they could obtain, and were forced to offer dozens of times the original price of the shares to cover those sales. As the old rhyme goes, "He who sells what isn't his'n/Must buy it back or go to prison."

Are there any restrictions on short selling other than margin requirements?

Yes. There are rules, for securities sold on stock exchanges and in certain other circumstances, that prohibit short selling a security if the price of the security is declining in the market. The rules on this are quite technical and depend not only on the price of the immediately preceding trade but on the next preceding trade. One simple example of the rule is that you cannot sell short if the last trade was at a price lower than the next preceding trade. The purpose of this rule is to help prevent the price of securities in a declining market from being driven even further down by short selling.

Can anybody engage in short selling so long as he or she has a margin account?

No, certain insiders and large shareholders of publicly held corporations are, under section 16 of the Securities

Exchange Act of 1934, prohibited except under very limited circumstances from selling short virtually any equity security issued by their company. The persons involved are generally officers, directors, and shareholders who own beneficially more than 10 percent of one of a publicly held company's equity securities. There are many tricks involved here, though, including with the definition of "officer" and in the calculation of the percentage of beneficial ownership.

Who receives any dividends paid on stocks that I have sold short?

Whoever buys the shares in the trading markets from the short seller will receive dividends just the way any other owner does. That is because, from a purchaser's standpoint, there is no difference in buying securities that were sold by a short seller and those that were sold in the usual way. The lender of the securities does not receive a dividend from the corporation that issued the securities because the lender no longer owns the securities. However, an amount equal to the dividend that would have been paid to the lender of the securities is taken out of your account and put in the lender's account. If this were not done, the lender would not be made whole by your simply buying securities in the market later and giving them to the lender to cover your short sale.

What are the main reasons for selling short?

Usually, people sell short because they believe the market price will decline and they will be able to make money by covering their short sale at a lower price. Sometimes people sell short because they want to get out of the market on securities they own at the current price, but for some reason they are unable to deliver the securities at the time of sale. For example, they may have lost their stock certificate and have not yet been able to replace it. Or, they may have pledged their stock to a bank as security for a loan and, as is always the case, they will then have delivered their stock certificate to the bank as security for the loan. Among other reasons, people also sometimes sell short for tax reasons.

What is a tax reason for selling short?

One tax reason, at least, is to shift the year in which you recognize profit on a sale for tax purposes. Say, for example, that, in December of a particular year, you want to lock in the current price of a stock you own and want to sell, but you don't want to realize any gain until the next year. To do that you could sell the stock short. As indicated above, this is called selling short "against the box." In January of the next year you could, working through your broker, close out both of your positions in the stock (in market parlance you will be both short and long in the stock) by delivering the shares you own to whomever the shares were borrowed from. What you will have ended up doing is shifting your gain from one year to the other.

Why would I want to shift the year in which my gain is recognized?

You may wish to do that for a number of reasons. These would vary by situation, but a couple of the common reasons would be these. First, you may expect to be in a lower tax bracket the next year. Second, you can earn interest on the amount of the tax that has been pushed over into the succeeding year.

Confirmations

What kind of confirmation should I get that an order has been executed?

You should receive a confirming telephone call from your broker the same day you make a trade. In this call, the broker can be expected to pass on the price at which the securities were bought or sold, along with the total amount you owe in the case of a purchase. In addition, a written confirmation should be mailed within a day or two after an order is executed.

What should I do when I receive oral and written confirmations?

You should carefully check the information you are given in both oral and written confirmations, and immediately notify your broker if an order was not executed correctly, or if there is some other problem. Notes taken at the time an order was placed will be especially useful not only in this checking, but as evidence of a problem. Unless a problem is taken care of immediately, it may be difficult or impossible to correct it later. You should keep any notes and written confirmations at least until you have compared them to information appearing on your monthly or quarterly statements from your brokerage firm. (This will be discussed further in chapter 7.)

Paying for Securities

When do I have to pay for securities I buy?

For almost all transactions, you must pay for securities purchased within five business days, and this means getting a check into the brokerage firm's hands on that day, not mailing it that day. This requirement is not affected by the fact that you may not have received a written confirmation within five business days. The date upon which payment must be made, which is called the "settlement date," is only one business day in the case of certain securities, such as U.S. government securities.

WORKING WITH YOUR BROKER

What should my approach be when my broker suggests that I buy a particular stock?

At least until you get to know your broker very well, I suggest you take your broker's recommendations to buy securities the way you would take the recommendations of any salesperson about his or her product. As discussed above, brokers are not analysts, and there is no particular reason to believe that your broker can on his or her own pick stocks any better than you can. To find out what's behind a broker's recommendation, you will need to ask some questions.

What kind of questions should I ask a broker about a buy recommendation?

You should ask questions that uncover where the recommendation came from, why it was made, and when it was made. If it came from the firm's research department, there may be a written report, and if you have any interest in the recommendation, you would be wise to ask for a copy of the report. Other things being equal, the more recent the recommendation, the better. If much time has passed since the firm made a buy recommendation, the market probably has already risen in response to anything in the report. You also may want to ask the broker what other stocks the research department recommends that are in the same general category as the stock the broker has recommended. If you are going to ask for a copy of the research report on the stock your broker called you about, you probably would be wise to see reports on competing stocks that the firm's analysts have reported on.

In general, you should ask your broker questions designed to see if a stock he or she recommends fits your basic investment objectives. If you have told your broker in the past that you are interested in buying safe stocks to put away for your retirement, and your broker has called to suggest buying a speculative stock in a new company, there is no sense talking further about the broker's recommendation. What you need to do at that point, of course, is think seriously about whether you need a new broker.

What are some other things I should watch out for in a broker's recommendations?

Probably the biggest thing to watch out for is a recommendation that promises, or comes close to promising, a sure thing. "Sure things" to buy or sell are very rare in investing. If your broker tells you he or she has one, the broker probably is exaggerating mightily or is incompetent. Once in a while, however, a broker may have a recommmendation that is close to being a sure thing.

I am not here referring to brokers who pass on information from an insider in a company that, when later announced, will almost certainly cause the stock's price to rise or fall. Don't bite on information your broker says or intimates comes from an insider. First, trading on inside information is illegal. If a broker's tip is illegal and you buy based on it, you could be in deep legal trouble. Second, if it's not an illegal tip but merely something based on rumor, it probably isn't any good and you should expect to lose money. (See chapter 12 for a discussion of insider trading.)

There is, however, one time when a broker's buy recommmendation is very close to a sure thing, and legal too.

When might a broker call me with a recommendation that is both legal and very close to a sure thing?

There is something called a "hot issue." If a broker calls you about one of these, listen carefully.

What is a hot issue?

A hot issue occurs sometimes in connection with a registered public offering of a company that previously was not publicly held. In a registered public offering, a company registers securities with the Securities and Exchange Commission, and with state securities agencies, for sale to the public and then sells those securities through securities firms. Occasionally, the securities firms marketing the securities find out during the registration process that there is an extraordinary demand for the securities that cannot be met by the number of securities the company is willing to sell. The first thing that happens then is that the company and the securities firms decide to raise the price of the securities above what they originally planned. Usually, that brings demand in line with supply and so, in the end, there is no extraordinary demand. Once in a very great while, however, the price is not raised enough to cool the demand and the securities firms that are going to sell these securities know to a virtual certainty that there are still more people who want to buy than there are securities available. Immediately after a public offering, the securities that are sold in the offering begin trading in the ordinary trading market. When there is more demand for a security than there are securities available, it is almost certain that the price of the security will rise in the trading market. This is the classic hot issue.

Who gets to buy securities that are to be sold in a hot issue?

When a securities firm has securities to sell in a hot issue, the firm's brokers, or at least some of them, are allotted a certain limited number of shares that they can sell to their favored customers. If your broker tells you he or she has a hot issue, ask enough questions to make sure your broker is describing a real hot issue and is not simply misusing the term. Among other things, you should ask how many shares your broker can sell. If the number is unlimited, it's not a hot issue.

I hear a lot about penny stocks. What is a penny stock, and what if my broker recommends one?

Basically, a penny stock is a stock that originally sells for less than $5 (and often less than $1) and that is issued by a small company with prospects that are, at best, uncertain. These stocks tend to be sold initially and then later traded by certain brokerage firms, and their traditional target is the unsophisticated investor looking to make a quick killing in the stock market. The penny stock area has had more than its share of shady operators and outright crooks, and it has recently come under special regulation by Congress and the Securities and Exchange Commission. It's true that you sometimes can make a lot of money in the penny stock market, but before getting involved ask yourself whether what attracts you is the straight gamble. If that's it, I suggest you go to Las Vegas instead. At least there you could watch good shows while you lose your money.

What should I do when I get a "cold call" from a broker I don't know?

While certain old-line brokerage firms have taken to making cold calls, seemingly indiscriminately to people whose names they get from some mailing list, many such calls come from people who only purport to be brokers. Most of their deals are pure scams. Considering just the difficulty of separating reputable callers from crooks, I can see no reason why you should invest with anyone who simply calls you on the telephone. Stick with brokers you know.

BUYING STOCKS DIRECTLY FROM COMPANIES (OR FROM THE SECURITIES FIRMS THAT HELP THEM SELL)

Registered Public Offerings

What is a registered public offering?

In a registered public offering, a company registers with the Securities and Exchange Commission, and state securities agencies, securities that it or one or more of its major shareholders wishes to sell. Registered public offerings are done because, under the Securities Act of 1933 and most states' laws, companies and their major shareholders generally may not legally sell securities to the public without registration. In most cases, the securities are wholesaled to a syndicate of securities firms that immediately resell the securities either to the public or to other securities firms that resell to the public.

From an investor's standpoint, how does buying securities in a registered public offering differ from buying them in the usual way from a securities firm?

Usually when you buy securities through a securities firm, the securities are purchased in the trading market, and you pay a brokerage commission for the transaction. There are no commissions in registered public offerings, because the securities firms make their profit from buying the securities wholesale and then reselling them at retail. Another major difference is that, in a registered public offering, purchasers are given a document, called a prospectus, that describes the company and the securities being sold. Depending on the kind of company involved, the prospectus may run anywhere from a few pages to over fifty.

In many cases the company selling the securities in a registered public offering has not previously had its securities owned by the public. That type of offering is called an initial public offering, or IPO. In an initial public offering there will be relatively little information publicly available about the company, except through the prospectus. It is important to understand that, in an initial public offering, the market will not previously have set a price on the company's securities. The price you pay, therefore, is one that the company and the securities firms doing the selling merely believe will be maintained in the trading market after the initial public offering is over.

Are there any benefits to buying in a registered public offering?

The price you pay can be a beneficial one. As indicated above, you do not pay a commission on the purchase. Also, in an initial public offering, the company and the securities firms involved in the deal typically try very hard to price the securities low enough so that the price will at least remain stable — and, they hope, go up — in the trading market that will follow.

Under the securities laws, purchasers in the public offering, and also purchasers who later buy in the trading market, can sue to get their money back, or for damages if they have already sold their securities, whenever securities are sold in a registered public offering by means of a prospectus that contains any material misstatement or omission. Everyone involved with a public offering knows that if the price of the securities falls in the trading market, lawyers representing plaintiffs will read the prospectus very carefully to try to find a statement that may be materially defective. Besides carefully drafting the prospectus in an initial public offering, the best way to avoid a lawsuit is to price the securities low enough that the price will not go down in the trading market.

A benefit of buying in an initial public offering is that it can be a good opportunity to get in early on a company that may have a promising future. The important word to focus on in that last sentence, however, is "may." Often shares bought in an initial public offering don't turn out to be a great investment, especially in the long term when compared with other alternatives. Why does your broker suggest initial public offerings to you? One reason may be that his or her compensation for selling shares in an initial public offering is likely to be much higher than the usual broker's commission for a trading transaction. Also, your broker may be under at least subtle pressure by his or her firm to help sell the firm's allotment in the offering.

How do I find out about registered public offerings?

Typically investors find out about registered public offerings through their broker, although they may read about such offerings in a newspaper or magazine. The *Wall Street Journal* is often filled with advertisements, called tombstone advertisements because of their stylized format, for securities being sold in registered public offerings. Tombstone advertisements typically appear on the day after the selling of the securities begins. If you call your broker after seeing the advertisement, the securities probably will already have been sold if the offering has been a popular one. In that case, your broker can buy the securities for you in the trading market, but you may have to pay a higher price, along with a commission.

Why do you mention only tombstone advertisements for registered public offerings? Aren't I likely to see advertising that provides details about the offerings?

The securities laws severely limit the ability of companies and securities firms to advertise securities for sale in registered public offerings (and in other circumstances as well). For this reason, the only advertisement you are likely to see in a registered public offering is the tombstone advertisement.

Are there special things I need to look out for when buying securities in an initial public offering?

Typically the biggest danger in an initial public offering is that the price of the securities has been set too high to be maintained in the trading market. One danger sign of bad pricing is if the securities are slow to sell in the registered offering. The longer the offering takes to sell out, the more wary you should be. If it has not sold out completely by the end of the second day, I think you should be very wary.

There is one trap you can fall into here, and you need to avoid it. A trading market will develop almost immediately after selling in the initial public offering has begun, because some people who purchase in a public offering change their mind about the securities almost immediately and want to resell. You may think that you can have your broker check the price in the trading market, during the period when the public offering is still going on, to see if the price has gone down in the trading market. You can have your broker check the price in the trading market, but the information you'll get will be worthless. That's because the securities firms in charge of the public offering will have stabilized the price in the trading market.

What does it mean to stabilize a price in the trading market?

During the period when securities remain unsold in a registered public offering, the securities firms involved in the selling effort place a bid in the trading market to buy the securities at or very near the price in the public offering. They do that to prevent the price in the trading market from dropping below the price in the registered offering, because if the price dropped, they would not be able, as a practical matter, to sell the securities at the public offering price. Stabilizing is a form of market manipulation, and market manipulation is blatantly illegal in most cases. The Securities Exchange Act of 1934, however, makes an exception for stabilizing during a registered public offering. The long and short of it, for an investor, is that the price in the trading market cannot be trusted to tell you anything until after the public offering is over.

What else do I have to look out for in a registered public offering?

You will, of course, want to evaluate the offering carefully to see if the securities being offered meet your investment objectives. In the typical offering, most of the selling effort actually goes on during the period when the registration statement for the securities is waiting to be declared effective by the Securities and Exchange Commission. During that period, what is called a preliminary prospectus should be sent to you by your broker if you have shown an interest in buying the securities (more colorfully, your broker will send you a red herring, which is what a preliminary prospectus is called because of the red legends it traditionally has carried on its front cover). This document will have some blanks in it, for example, the exact price to be charged probably will not be stated, but the document will be very helpful for evaluating the offering.

The prospectus in its final form will not be available until after the securities are registered and, in the usual offering, the securities will be sold before the average investor has time to see the final prospectus. It will be sent to purchasers, however, at least by the time they receive a written confirmation of sale.

What are some of the things I should look for in preliminary and final prospectuses?

You should read a prospectus with at least three general questions in mind. First, does the prospectus describe a company you wish to invest in? Second, does the type of security offered meet your investment objectives? Third, is the deal offered on the security a good one? When you read a prospectus, remember that it is viewed in the securities industry largely as a device to protect against liability by disclosing all the problems that could occur in the investment. Because of that, the prospectus will be anything but upbeat.

Toward the front of many prospectuses, you will find a section detailing risk factors. You should pay particular attention to what the company has to say there. The prospectus also will contain detailed financial statements, which will be worth your special effort. In reading the financial statements, make sure you examine the notes that accompany them and also pay particular attention to the section of the prospectus that contains management's discussion and analysis of the company's financial condition and the results of its operations. The Securities and Exchange Commission has pushed companies hard to make that discussion and analysis helpful to investors.

What should I do with the preliminary and final prospectuses after I'm done with them?

You should keep the preliminary and final prospectuses, along with anything else you are given in writing about a registered public offering. You also should keep any notes you took when you discussed the offering with your broker. If the price of the securities goes down, you may have a legal claim under federal law based, among other things, on material misrepresentations or omissions in the prospectus, or in other communications in connection with the offering. (Information is material in this context if there is a substantial likelihood that a reasonable investor would attach importance to it in determining whether to purchase the security being offered.) You also may have claims under state law.

Dividend-Reinvestment Plans

What is a dividend-reinvestment plan?

A dividend-reinvestment plan is a plan established by a publicly held company that allows shareholders automatically to buy shares of the company's stock with their dividends. Only some corporations pay dividends, but a number of those that do have dividend-reinvestment plans.

How does an investor sign up for a dividend-reinvestment plan?

Companies that offer such plans periodically send information to their shareholders along with forms that can be filled out to take advantage of the plan. In addition, your broker should be able to check for you to see if a particular corporation has such a plan. Alternatively, you could call the company yourself to check. Merely get the telephone number for the company's headquarters and tell the person who answers the phone you want to speak with the shareholder relations department. Once you know a company has such a plan, you can ask its shareholder relations department to provide you with the necessary form for signing up. Note, however, that you probably will not be able to take advantage of a dividend-reinvestment plan if you hold your securities in "Street name."

Are dividend-reinvestment plans a good deal?

Providing further investment in the company's stock fits with your financial plan, and as long as the price of the securities continues to be acceptable to you, the plan typically offers one major benefit. That is, you usually either pay no commission or only a small commission to purchase the securities. Also, dividend-reinvestment plans can be an easy way to increase the size of your holdings in that you do not have to bother with the details of placing an order and then sending a check to your broker.

Does an investor still have to pay income tax on dividends that are subject to a dividend-reinvestment plan?

Yes, there is no escaping the income tax on dividends. It has to be paid even though an investor never physically sees the cash from the dividend.

Rights Offerings

What is a rights offering?

In a rights offering, a company makes an offer to each of its shareholders to sell to them a certain number of shares of the company's stock at a specified price. The number of shares offered is in proportion to the shares already owned, for example five shares offered for every one hundred shares owned.

What is the reason behind rights offerings?

In some corporations, shareholders have what are called preemptive rights. Sometimes those rights are mandated by the law of the state in which the corporation is incorporated. A preemptive right gives shareholders the right, under most circumstances, to maintain their proportionate ownership in a corporation when new shares are sold. If a corporation has preemptive rights, a rights offering will be necessary before the company can sell new shares to the public. More typically, however, companies do rights offerings either because they believe such offerings are good ways to raise capital, because they believe the offerings are good for shareholder relations, or for a combination of those reasons.

Are there any benefits to the investor in a rights offering?

In a rights offering, a shareholder will be able to buy shares without paying a brokerage commission. Also, the price may be somewhat more favorable than one can obtain in the public market. If so, the rights themselves have value, and a trading market will develop for the rights, allowing shareholders to sell them if they do not want to use them to buy more shares. For the typical investor, being able to maintain his or her proportionate ownership in a publicly held company is completely irrelevant. Preemptive rights really make sense only for privately owned corporations or for major shareholders of publicly held corporations.

Private Placements and Other Exempt Offerings

What is an exempt offering?

An exempt offering is an offering of securities that is exempt from the registration requirements of the securities laws. Under the Securities Act of 1933, and under the laws of virtually all states, securities must be registered with the Securities and Exchange Commission, and the relevant state securities agency, before they may be sold, except if an exemption from the registration requirement is available. Note that such an offering is exempt only from the registration requirements, not from the other provisions of the securities laws, such as provisions that protect investors from buying securities based on false and misleading statements or as a result of fraudulent acts.

What kinds of exempt offerings are there?

There are a wide variety of exempt offerings under federal law, and even more under the laws of the various states. A few of the more common under federal law are the regulation A offering, private-placement and intrastate offerings, and the offerings made under regulation D and rule 701.

What is a regulation A offering?

A regulation A offering is an offering that follows the requirements of regulation A under the Securities Act of 1933. It is an exempt offering, but to the average investor it looks more like a registered public offering than anything else. So much is that the case that a regulation A offering has traditionally been called by those in the securities industry a short-form registration. A nice thing about a regulation A offering, from the standpoint of investors, is that securities purchased in such an offering are not subject to the resale limitations under federal law, discussed below, on so-called restricted securities. There are no qualification requirements that offerees or purchasers must meet in a regulation A offering.

What is a private placement?

A private placement is an exempt offering under section 4(2) of the Securities Act of 1933. Basically, it is an offering to financial institutions or individuals who meet certain requirements. The most basic of these requirements are sufficient sophistication with respect to business and finance to be able to evaluate the offering and the ability to bear the financial risks of the offering. Another requirement is that offerees generally must be given the same kind of information they would get if the offering were a registered public offering. Private placements may be made only to people who are able to fend for themselves and who do not need the protections offered by the registration requirements of the securities laws. For offerings to individuals, other than people in very special relationships to the company (such as high company officers), offerees in private placements must be given a good deal of information about the company and the offering. Typically, they are given a document that looks very much like a prospectus in a registered public offering.

What are regulation D offerings?

Regulation D is a regulation under the Securities Act of 1933. It offers exemptions under three separate rules, rules 504, 505, and 506. Companies that follow the details of rule 506 will be deemed to have met the requirements of the private-placement exemption just discussed. Many of the details relate to who can be sold securities under rule 506, and to the information with which purchasers must be provided. Rule 505 has much in common with rule 506, but the requirements are not so stringent, and a dollar limit of $5 million has been added. Rule 504 essentially calls for only the filing of a simple form by the issuer with the Securities and Exchange Commission. (So lax is the rule, in fact, that an issuer can get the benefits of the rule even if it willfully ignores the filing requirement.) However, only up to $1 million of securities may be sold under rule 504 in a twelve-month period, and the rule isn't usable by publicly held companies or some other kinds of companies. A benefit to purchasers in rule 504 offerings is that the securities purchased (at least since August 13, 1992) are not subject to the resale limitations on restricted securities under federal law. State law, however, may be another story.

What is a rule 701 offering?

Rule 701 (under the Securities Act of 1933) offerings are made to employees, officers, directors, or certain other people having close relationships with a privately owned company. The offerings must be made pursuant to a written compensatory benefit plan or contract. Common examples are profit-sharing and stock option or stock purchase plans. Depending on the circumstances, from $500,000 to $5 million of securities may be sold under rule 701 within a twelve-month period. The other requirements for these offerings are quite lenient. There is, for example, no requirement that someone buying in a rule 701 offering have any sophistication with respect to business or finance, or even be able to understand and evaluate the offering.

What is an intrastate offering?

Basically, an intrastate offering is an offering that is made only to persons who are "residents" of a single state or territory, where the issuer of the security is a "resident" of and does at least the bulk of its business within that state or territory. The intrastate offering is allowed to be done without registration by section 3(a)(11) of the Securities Act of 1933. A company can simply follow the statute itself or it can take advantage of the so-called safe-harbor provisions of rule 147. This offering is very tricky for various reasons, including that it has special definitions of the terms "resident" and "doing business."

What are some of the common issues involved in exempt offerings?

One thing that all of these offerings have in common is the fact that, if the company selling the securities fouls up the requirements or exceeds the limitations of the offering, the offering is illegal under the Securities Act of 1933. In the case of an offering that is not exempt from the Act's registration requirements, section 12(1) of the Act gives purchasers the right to get their money back or, if they have already sold their securities before bringing suit, they have a right to damages. Note that for most of these offerings, the securities may be offered and sold only to people who meet certain requirements. In a properly done such offering, the people selling the securities will make sure offerees know what those requirements are and, in addition, will require purchasers to certify that they meet those requirements. Be very careful that you do not say that you meet requirements you do not meet. Sometimes people selling the securities are more interested in selling than in doing the job right. They may even encourage you to sign a document saying you meet requirements you don't meet. That can get them into trouble, but you need to realize that you can be in big legal trouble for making false representations in that situation. You may even be financially responsible for any money you cost the company by fouling up the offering. Do not under any circumstances represent that you meet requirements you do not meet. Also, do not sign a paper saying that you have been given certain information if you have not been given it.

Are there benefits to purchasing in an exempt offering?

Exempt offerings often allow investors to buy securities that are not generally available to the public. Sometimes this is an opportunity to get in on the ground floor of a company that may in the future become large and profitable. In any case, because you are given an opportunity not available generally, these often are opportunities worth looking at. However, exempt offerings need to be looked at very carefully. You want to make sure, of course, that you are not being taken in by a scam. You want to make sure that you have faith in the people who are behind the company. You want to be sure you understand the company's business and have faith in its prospects, and that you understand the risks involved in the investment.

Are there some special detriments to buying securities in exempt offerings?

Restrictions on the transfer of the securities you buy stand out in my mind as a special problem. In most instances, securities purchased in exempt offerings may not be freely resold. The documents you are given in connection with the offering should spell out the basic restrictions on transfer. In most cases, the securities you purchase will be called "restricted securities." Restricted securities may not be resold publicly until a number of requirements are met, including a holding period of at least two years in almost all cases.

Securities purchased in intrastate offerings have their own set of restrictions, including that they may not be resold to people who do not meet specified requirements with respect to residence in the state in which the securities were sold until some period has passed, typically either nine months or one year.

In addition to those types of legal restrictions on transfer, in most cases when you buy securities in exempt offerings, you buy them from privately held companies. In other words, there typically is not a public market for the securities and, even when you could sell them legally in some circumstances, you may find that you will have trouble finding a buyer. Any certificates for securities you purchase in most exempt offerings should have on them a legend noting in general terms the restrictions on transfer. (Putting that legend on is called "legending" the stock.) If the company is handling matters the way it should, it will not allow such a certificate to be transferred into someone else's name until it is satisfied that all of the legal requirements for a transfer have been met.

I might mention that, in the case of restricted securities, you could under some circumstances transfer those securities without meeting the ordinary holding requirement. Basically, this usually would entail at least offering and selling the securities only to people who meet certain requirements with respect to sophistication in business and finance and ability to bear risk. All this is very complicated.

In short, if you purchase securities in the kind of exempt offering discussed above (other than, at least insofar as federal law is concerned, a regulation A or rule 504 offering), do not attempt to resell them, even to the point of discussing a possible purchase with someone you hope to sell them to, without checking with a securities lawyer. Not only will that save you from getting into trouble, but it will smooth the way for your being able to sell. Before the company will lift restrictions on resale it will, if its people know what they are doing, require a number of things from you and, as a practical matter, the company most likely will want to work through your lawyer. Restrictions on resale are discussed further in chapter 12.

What if I buy securities not from the company that issued them or through a brokerage firm, but directly from the person who owns them; are there legal limitations on my ability to resell the securities?

There may or may not be resale limitations in that circumstance, depending on a whole series of variables. For one thing, the securities may or may not be restricted securities. Unless resale limitations are clearly laid out for you in a particular deal, the smart thing to do is run the resale question by a lawyer before you buy. Resale limitations definitely should affect the price you pay for securities.

What records should I keep in connection with an exempt offering?

You should keep anything given to you in writing, along with a note as to when it was given to you, by whom, and under what circumstances. You also should keep notes on what was told to you orally, including by whom and when and under what circumstances. These records could be critically important if problems arise with the investment in the future.

What protections do I have in the event of problems with the investment?

As indicated above, if securities are sold without registration and registration was required, each purchaser has the right to get his or her money back or, if the securities have been sold, damages. About the only requirement under federal law is that the action be brought within the statute of limitations, which usually would expire one year after the violation on which the action is based.

Also, if the securities were sold based on material misstatements or omissions, an investor has the right to get his or her money back, or damages if the securities have already been sold. Under federal law, those actions have to be brought within one to three years, depending on the circumstances.

Under other provisions of the securities laws, purchasers who are cheated by fraudulent acts also have additional remedies.

CHAPTER

6

About Bonds

TYPES OF BONDS AND WHERE TO BUY THEM

What types of bonds are available for purchase by investors?

A large number of corporations issue bonds of various types. The federal government, and several federal agencies, issue a wide variety of bonds, as do state and municipal governments and different types of state and local agencies.

What kinds of bonds are available from corporations?

Bonds and debentures, which can be viewed as a type of bond, were discussed briefly in chapter 5. One way to categorize corporate bonds is by the degree of risk involved with them. Many old-line American corporations have traditionally issued bonds of high investment quality, offering relatively modest interest rates with relatively great security. During the decade of the 1980s, many other corporations began issuing riskier bonds with relatively high interest rates, which are called junk bonds (people who like them call them high-yield securities). During the 1980s junk bonds usually were issued in connection with some kind of corporate takeover. In the 1990s junk bonds typically are being issued to refinance earlier junk bond offerings that carried higher interest rates. In addition to bonds issued originally as junk bonds, there is another kind of junk bond: the fallen angel. Fallen angels are bonds that only became junk bonds when their issuer fell on hard times. What junk bonds all have in common is that they offer high investment risk and high interest payments.

What kind of bonds does the U.S. government itself issue?

The U.S. government issues savings bonds, and they can be purchased at most banks. The U.S. government bonds you hear more about are Treasury bonds, which are sold directly by the government through the Federal Reserve system along with Treasury notes and Treasury bills.

How do Treasury bonds, Treasury notes, and Treasury bills differ?

There are other differences between these securities, such as the minimum denominations available for each, but the overwhelmingly important difference is their maturity. Treasury bills mature in either three months, six months, or one year; Treasury notes mature in from two to ten years; and Treasury bonds have maturities of over ten years, with the maximum being thirty years. All of these securities are backed by what is called the "full faith and credit" of the U.S. government.

How can I buy Treasury bonds, Treasury notes, and Treasury bills?

All of these securities can be purchased directly from one of the Federal Reserve Banks that have offices around the country, and you can also buy them from the Federal Reserve system by mail and from the Treasury Department under a program called the Direct Book Entry Security System. Under that system accounts are set up for investors and interest payments are made directly to the investors' banks. It is possible to buy those securities by bidding for them against other investors. To do this you have to bid based on what yield you will accept. Very few individual investors involve themselves in the competitive bidding process. Rather, they simply buy securities having a yield that is set as a result of the bidding process engaged in by others. For $4.50 you can buy from the Federal Reserve system a booklet entitled *Buying Treasury Securities at Federal Reserve Banks*. Write to:

> Federal Reserve Bank of Richmond
> P.O. Box 27471
> Richmond, VA 23261

You can get information about buying these securities direct from the Treasury Department by calling (202) 874-4000, pressing 1, then 233. You will hear a message about the Treasury Department's program. You then can press 1, then 241, to leave your name and address. Further information will then be sent to you. You also can buy these securities through your broker, although that involves paying a commission.

What about bonds issued by federal agencies?

A number of federal agencies issue bonds of various types. Securities issued by federal agencies can be purchased either through the Federal Reserve system or through brokerage firms.

What about municipal bonds?

The term "municipal bond" is somewhat of a misnomer, since many of the bonds people call municipal bonds are in fact issued not by municipalities but by other governmental entities at the state or local level. A major breakdown of municipal bonds is between general obligation bonds, which are backed by the taxing power of the issuer, and bonds issued by such agencies as industrial development authorities that are not backed by taxing authority. Yet another way to break down municipal bonds is between those that are free from federal, and often state and local, taxation and those that are taxable. The rules for determining whether municipal bonds are free from federal income tax are tricky. What the average investor who seeks tax-free bonds needs to do is make sure that the particular issue of bonds being purchased is free from tax. Typically, municipal bonds that are free from federal income taxes are also free from state and local taxes in the state of issuance. One typically buys municipal bonds through a brokerage firm.

What are zero-coupon bonds?

A zero-coupon bond is a bond that pays its principal amount upon maturity, but does not pay any interest before then. Zero-coupon bonds are sold at large discounts from their face value, so the increase from what you pay to the face value is, in effect, the interest payback. Corporations sometimes issue zero-coupon bonds, but at least currently the U.S. government does not. Brokerage firms, however, sometimes "strip" the right to receive interest payments from government bonds and then sell the right to receive interest payments separately from the stripped bonds.

What are convertible bonds and what are income bonds?

These types of bonds are, in a sense, hybrids between straight debt securities and equity securities. A convertible bond is a bond that is convertible into the common stock of the corporation that issues it, or perhaps into the corporation's preferred stock. A bond convertible into common stock allows the investor to collect interest relatively securely, but it also allows the investor to share in the issuer's successes if the company's common stock increases in value to a specified point. In that case, the bond holder can convert the bond into stock on a basis that is spelled out in the bond.

With an income bond, the interest on the bond is payable only if the company has earnings out of which the interest can be paid. Unlike the usual bond, the interest on an income bond is not an absolute debt of the corporation. For this reason, the interest rate payable on an income bond has to be higher than it would be on an ordinary bond, other things being equal. Neither convertible bonds nor income bonds are common.

CHARACTERISTICS OF BONDS

In what form does an investor take title to a bond?

Traditionally, bonds were issued either as registered bonds or as bearer bonds. A registered bond, like common or preferred stock, is registered on the books of the issuer in the name of the owner. Bearer bonds, on the other hand, are not registered in anyone's name, but rather are payable to whoever presents them for payment. The interest on registered bonds is sent to the registered owner. Bearer bonds have coupons attached to them that are clipped and presented for payment whenever interest payments are due, usually semi-annually. There are still a lot of bearer bonds in the hands of investors, but in recent years only registered bonds have been issued. The movement away from bearer bonds was not mandated by the interest of investors, but rather by the demand of the Internal Revenue Service that bonds be issued in a form that would allow it to know who is paid the interest. For the average investor not interested in committing tax fraud, there is no reason to mourn the passing of bearer bonds. They're a real pain to deal with.

How are bonds rated for safety?

Various rating agencies rate bonds for safety. The best known are Moody's and Standard & Poor's. Each of these agencies rates bonds starting with Aaa for Moody's and

AAA for Standard & Poor's, and going through AA to A, to BBB, to BB, and so on. Your broker can tell you the ratings of various bonds you may be interested in. As might be expected, the higher the rating, the lower the yield to the investor.

What is a coupon rate?

The coupon rate is the interest rate that is specified on the bond. It does not matter whether the bond actually is a bearer bond having coupons.

What does par value mean in terms of bonds?

Bonds are almost always issued in denominations of $1,000 or a multiple thereof. The par value of such a bond is said to be $1,000.

What are premiums and discounts on bonds?

A premium is any price in excess of the bond's par value, usually $1,000. A bond selling at less than par is said to be selling at a discount.

What is the yield to maturity of a bond?

The yield to maturity of a bond is the rate of return an investor will receive, on average, if the bond is held from the date of purchase to the date of maturity. If a bond is purchased at par, the yield to maturity would be equal to the coupon rate. The yield to maturity would differ from the coupon rate if the bond is purchased at either a discount from or a premium over par. In addition to other factors, bond prices go up and down in response to changes in general interest rates. If, for example, general interest rates are 6 percent and a bond issued some years ago has a coupon rate of 9 percent, the bond can be expected to trade at a premium, which would make the yield to maturity closer to 6 percent than to 9 percent.

What is the current yield on a bond?

The current yield on a bond is the return an investor can get currently, in terms of interest, relative to the current market price of the bond. If the current price of the bond is $1,000, the current yield would be equal to the coupon rate. If the bond is currently selling at a discount or a premium, however, the current yield would be either higher or lower than the coupon rate.

What is a sinking fund for bonds?

Under the terms of some bonds, the corporation that issues the bonds must set aside in a special account a specified amount of money each year in order to ensure that funds will be available to repay the bonds at their maturity. Bonds with sinking funds are obviously safer than bonds without, although in the case of a great many corporations sinking funds are not really necessary for investors to feel a high degree of confidence that the corporation will be able to repay the bonds at maturity. One reason for that confidence is that corporations usually have no problem issuing new bonds to get funds to repay old bonds. So long as the company remains strong, that sort of refinancing is not a problem.

What does it mean for a bond to be callable?

A callable bond is one that can be paid off before maturity by the corporation that issued it. This is very much like the repayment provision one virtually always has on a home mortgage. Typically you can pay your mortgage in accordance with the payment schedule, over perhaps fifteen to thirty years, or you can repay the mortgage loan early. Typically, bonds that are callable have a "no-call" feature for a limited period, such as five years. Investors like a no-call provision because it allows them to plan on receiving a set amount of interest at least for a limited time.

What happens to the interest that has accrued on a bond, but has not been paid, at the time a bond is sold in the trading market?

When an investor sells a bond in the trading market, the interest accrued to date is calculated, and the purchaser of the bond pays to the seller an amount equal to the accrued interest.

Part III

LIVING WITH
INVESTMENTS

Once an investor is set up with investment professionals and has made investments, he or she enters a period of living with those investments. Except for deciding when to sell the investments, it may seem at first glance that living with investments is a purely passive matter. It may appear that all an investor needs to do is sit back and hope his or her investments increase in value, while collecting dividends and interest on investments that pay them. While that is true with some investments, typically the investor is faced with a number of situations during the course of an investment that require both understanding and decision. The purpose of this part of the book is to help provide some of that understanding, and also to aid investors in making the right decisions.

Some of the questions covered here relate to managing the details of your investments, such as recordkeeping and the safekeeping and delivery upon sale of stock certificates. Other questions relate to dividends, to the information you should receive from companies you invest in, and to proxy voting. Yet others cover mergers, tender offers, and stock repurchases and exchanges. This part of the book also gets into a variety of situations that put limitations on an investor's ability to resell securities (and also to buy them), including limitations that flow from the short-swing trading provisions of the Securities Exchange Act of 1934 and from the prohibitions on insider trading under rules 10b-5 and 14e-3.

C H A P T E R

7

Managing Details of Investments

MONTHLY AND QUARTERLY STATEMENTS

What should I look for on my monthly or quarterly statement from my brokerage firm?

If your securities are held in "Street name," make sure that the statement continues month after month to list the names of the securities you own, and in the correct amounts. Also, make sure that the statements correctly show any transactions that you engaged in during the period. The best way to do this typically is to compare the statements against the written confirmations of transactions that should have been sent to you promptly after your orders were executed.

If you own securities in "Street name," the brokerage firm will be paid any interest or dividends due to you. While it may be difficult for you to tell whether interest or dividends were properly credited to your account when you look at an individual monthly statement, you should check periodically to see that dividends and interest in the correct amounts appear on the proper periodic basis. If your account has a cash balance, check your current statement against the prior statement to make sure that cash has not disappeared mysteriously.

These are just examples. The important thing is to check whatever is necessary to see that the statement is correct in all particulars. (It is easy enough for a clerk to foul up and put the account in one name when the investor wants it in joint name with his or her spouse. Especially on your first statement, look carefully to see that the account is in the name or names you want it in.) It is obviously best for everyone if any mistakes are caught immediately. What is more important, if you catch a mistake sometime later, the brokerage firm may not be willing to correct it. In that case, you would have to go to arbitration or sue the firm and, depending on the type of problem and the length of the delay, an arbitrator or court may not be able to do anything about the problem. Among other problems, the statute of limitations may have run.

KEEPING RECORDS

What records should I keep about my investments?

You should keep your monthly or quarterly statements from your brokerage firm. You also should keep all confirmations of trades at least until you are sure that the trades correctly show in all necessary detail on the next statement. For example, for tax purposes when you sell, you will need to have an official record at least of the date of the transaction, the name of the security involved, the price at which you purchased or sold, and the brokerage commission. Frankly, I would suggest that unless your confirmation slips get too voluminous to store, you keep all of them along with your monthly statements.

In addition, you should keep as records anything that your brokerage firm sends you about your investments. You should keep copies of any letters or other written correspondence you send your brokerage firm. You also should keep any notes you take during relevant conversations with your broker or anyone else at the brokerage firm. One way to keep all these records is simply to have files set up by months. A better way is to keep monthly or quarterly statements in chronological order and keep other records in separate files each containing information about one security you own.

How long should I keep records?

Let me give an answer that may seem silly: you need to keep records as long as they may be relevant to something important. It is difficult to be more precise, because it is impossible to tell what later may be relevant. Certainly we know that taxes are due upon the sale of a security on which you have made a profit, and that you will want to establish a loss for tax purposes if you have sold securities at a loss. You need, therefore, to keep records of purchases not only until you have made sales and until those sales have shown up on your tax return, but until those tax returns are no longer subject to audit. Obviously, that means you need to keep records of all purchases for at least several years no matter how quickly you sell those securities, and, of course, you may need to keep the record of some purchases for decades. In terms of what might later be needed for arbitration of a problem or for the purposes of a lawsuit, records could conceivably be relevant, or even essential, for decades. Unless space for storing records gets to be a problem, you probably will find it easier to keep records than to go through them carefully and decide which you need and which you can afford to throw out.

HANDLING CERTIFICATES

Assuming I take title to securities in my own name and do not have my brokerage firm keep the certificates for me, how should I store the stock certificates and other securities that are sent me?

Unless you have in your home or office a fireproof safe that cannot easily be either opened or moved, I believe a safety deposit box is the place for your stock certificates and other securities. If you think a personal safe is the way to go, make sure you don't buy one that burglars can simply carry off. If you do, you can be sure it will be carried off if burglars can find it.

How should I deliver stock certificates or other securities to my brokerage firm after a sale?

If you have to deliver a stock certificate or other security to your brokerage firm after a sale, either hand deliver it or send it by registered mail. If you mail it, do not endorse it on the back and do not include in the same envelope an executed stock power (which is a form you can obtain from your broker that authorizes the transfer of the security). If you must send a stock power by mail, send it in a separate envelope. On the back of a stock certificate is a form that looks like a stock power, and you could simply sign the certificate on the back to authorize transfer. If your brokerage firm wishes you to do so, you can sign a certificate on the back if you hand deliver it.

You should never sign the certificate and mail it, however, even by registered mail. If a signed certificate were to fall into the hands of a thief or of someone who finds it if it is lost, the certificate could more easily be transferred to what is called a bona fide purchaser (legalese for an innocent purchaser who has taken without notice of a problem in the title to the securities), who could take legal ownership of the securities.

LOST, DESTROYED, OR STOLEN CERTIFICATES

What happens if one of my stock certificates is lost, destroyed, or stolen?

If one of your stock certificates is lost, destroyed, or stolen, you should call and then write the bank (or one of the banks) that is a transfer agent for the securities. The name of a bank and its city will appear on the stock certificates, and if you do not have another certificate for that same type of stock, your brokerage firm can get the information for you. (A transfer agent is simply a bank that handles the mechanics of stock transfers for the company that issues the securities.) As soon as the transfer agent gets notification from you that a stock certificate has been lost, destroyed, or stolen, it will put in its records a notation to stop the transfer of that certificate. Then if the certificate later is transferred when it shouldn't be, it will in most cases be the transfer agent's and the company's problem rather than yours. For this reason, it is important that you notify the transfer agent immediately, and you should do so by telephone followed immediately by a certified letter. (In your telephone call, check, by the way, to make sure that the bank hasn't been replaced as transfer agent.)

In your letter you should give all the information you gave in the telephone call, plus you should refer to the telephone call by date, time, and the name of the person you talked to. In the phone call and the letter, also request that a new certificate be issued to you, unless at this point you want to wait to see if the certificate turns up and if you are willing to run some additional risks if the old certificate ends up in the hands of a bona fide purchaser. (Waiting could save you the indemnity bond fee referred to in the answer to the next question, but I definitely wouldn't wait if you think the certificate might have been stolen, or if you're pretty sure it's been destroyed or lost for good.)

What will happen then? What else will I have to do to get a new certificate?

The transfer agent will send you forms to fill out, sign, and swear to before a notary. In those forms you will agree to indemnify the company that issued the securities and the transfer agent against any loss they may incur as a result of issuing you a new certificate. One of the forms you fill out will be an application for an indemnity bond whereby an insurance company agrees at least to pay for any loss of the transfer agent or the issuing company if you are not able to pay for the loss. The fee for that indemnity bond probably will be 3 percent of the market value of the securities involved. Note that the replacement of a stock certificate probably will take at least some weeks. Note also that you could be forced to give up your replacement certificate if the company is later forced to issue a new certificate to a bona fide purchaser who presents the old certificate.

CREDIT BALANCES

What happens to credit balances in my account at a brokerage firm?

What happens to your credit balances depends on what instructions you have given your brokerage firm. Brokerage firms are delighted to have you leave credit balances in your account. Sometimes these balances can get quite high, even if you have not sold securities to generate them, because of dividends or interest payments that may have been credited to the account. Unless you expect to place a buy order shortly and thus use the cash, or unless you need to keep the cash in your account to meet a margin requirement, I suggest that you have your account cleared of funds on a regular basis. You can instruct your brokerage firm to send you a check in the amount of your credit balance and, in addition, to do the same whenever a credit balance is available in the future. What may be a better idea for you is to have funds in your brokerage account automatically transferred to a money market account at your brokerage firm, preferably one that offers check-writing privileges.

CHAPTER

8

Dividends and Stock Splits

GENERAL DIVIDEND QUESTIONS

What are cash dividends?

From an investor's standpoint, a cash dividend is a payment by a corporation in cash to its shareholders, the amount of which is so much per share owned. Depending on the law of the state in which a corporation is incorporated, the dividend may be paid only from a corporation's earnings or, in some states, it may also be a return of money paid to the corporation by shareholders for their stock. The laws of some states require corporations to call the latter type of payments distributions, to distinguish them from payments made out of earnings.

It is important for investors to realize that the federal tax laws have their own definition of dividends; what is a cash dividend for income tax purposes may be quite different from what it is under state corporation law. Generally, if a corporation is repaying to shareholders some of the money that shareholders contributed in exchange for their stock, federal law will not tax the payment as a dividend. On the other hand, sometimes a corporation will do a distribution under state law out of funds originally contributed by shareholders, and yet tax law will treat the distribution as a taxable dividend. That typically would occur when a corporation has had earnings out of which it could have paid ordinary dividends but it has, for some reason or other, chosen to do a distribution.

Sometimes part of a corporation's cash dividend is taxable and some is not, the reason being that some of the cash is treated for tax purposes as being a return of the investment of shareholders. When a corporation pays a dividend that is nontaxable, in whole or in part, the corporation can be expected to inform the shareholders of that fact.

Do publicly held companies typically pay dividends?

Don't be fooled by the fact that most companies on the New York Stock Exchange pay dividends. Most publicly held corporations do not pay dividends. The companies that do pay dividends are generally the older, more established companies, which is why the percentages of companies paying are lower on the American Stock Exchange, lower yet on NASDAQ, and lowest on the other stocks traded over the counter. For companies that do pay dividends, the expectation of those payments plays a major role in setting the stock's price.

Why don't more companies pay dividends? Is it because they don't have the cash available?

Most companies do not pay dividends because their officers and directors, as well as their common shareholders, would rather see the company keep its cash and use it to make the business grow and become more profitable, because that will make the stock's price rise. A rise in the stock's price is what most shareholders want out of an investment, rather than a dividend. Further, until 1986 (and possibly in the future), capital gains on sales of stock were heavily favored by the tax laws, whereas dividends have always been ordinary income. The kinds of companies that pay dividends on their common stock are often mature companies, which, while relatively safe and stable, do not have much potential for major additional growth. The classic examples have been the utilities.

Can I rely on a company that has paid cash dividends to continue to pay them in set amounts?

Until a dividend is declared by a company's board of directors and announced publicly, the company is under no legal obligation to pay a red cent. However, companies that have traditionally paid dividends hate to miss paying a dividend or to lower dividends. Missing or lowering a dividend for such a company is a great blight on its record. Sometimes, of course, it's necessary, so dividends certainly cannot be relied upon, especially if a company's fortunes change. Note that what I have just said about a company not being required to pay dividends is as true of dividends on preferred stock as it is on common stock. In the case of preferred stock, however, a corporation's charter often contains provisions that give preferred shareholders certain rights if dividends are not paid in set amounts.

Record and Ex-Dividend Dates

What is the importance of a "record date" in connection with dividends?

Typically, in corporations that pay dividends, the board of directors will declare the dividends payable to all shareholders whose names appear on the company's books as shareholders at the close of business on a certain date in the future, which is called the "record date."

If I buy shares on the record date, will I receive the dividend?

No, and the explanation relates to the fact that, under usual business practices, purchasers of shares are given five business days to pay for the shares and sellers are given five business days to deliver the shares they have sold. What this comes down to, then, is that the date upon which you have to purchase shares if you are to receive the dividends on them is not the record date, but a date that, traditionally, is five business days prior to the record date. (The next day is called the ex-dividend date because purchasers of shares on and after that date will not have the right to receive the dividend.) Note that the market will adjust itself to take account of the fact that during some periods in a particular quarter the stock will carry with it the right to receive the quarterly dividend and during another period in the quarter the stock will not carry that right. If you do not know for sure whether you are going to receive a dividend on stock you purchase or sell, ask your broker to check. He or she can do so quite easily.

Dividends in Property

Do corporations ever pay dividends in property rather than cash?

As a matter of corporation law, corporations have the power to pay dividends in property rather than cash. This is rarely done, however, in publicly held corporations, but one sees it from time to time in privately owned corporations, especially when a corporation wishes to distribute its assets prior to dissolution. There is, however, one famous case of a publicly held corporation, whose business was distilling, that declared a dividend in property during World War II. The property involved was rights to buy whiskey at a wholesale price. Not only was that a way for thirsty shareholders to save money, it provided a way for them to get their hands on an extra stock of property that the war had made scarce.

Stock Dividends and Stock Splits

What about stock dividends?

The mechanics of declaring and paying a dividend in a corporation's own stock are essentially the same as for a cash dividend. The corporation might, for example, declare and pay a 5 percent stock dividend on its common stock. What would happen is that each shareholder would receive five additional shares for each one hundred previously owned.

What's the difference between a stock dividend and a stock split?

In a stock split, a corporation takes the proper legal action to divide its existing shares into a greater number of shares. If the stock has par value, in the pure stock split the par value of each share is reduced in proportion to the magnitude of the split. That is, if the stock originally has a par value of $1 and the company does a two-for-one stock split, the par value will become $0.50 per share. Notice that in this case the corporation will need to call back all of its existing stock certificates and issue new ones, since the par value showing on the old certificates will be incorrect after the split.

Does it make any difference to shareholders whether a corporation does a stock dividend or a stock split?

Especially since, as discussed in chapter 5, par value is essentially irrelevant to the average shareholder, the differences between stock splits and stock dividends are also essentially irrelevant to the average shareholder. In fact, a great many times when corporations announce stock splits they are actually, under corporation law, doing a stock dividend. One reason for this is that the accounting profession pushes corporations to use the term "stock split" except in the case of small percentage stock dividends.

Why do companies do stock splits or stock dividends?

Focusing only on publicly held companies, there are two basic reasons for doing stock splits or stock dividends. First, stock traditionally trades in certain price ranges. The stock of certain kinds of relatively new companies may, for example, trade traditionally between $10 and $50 per share, whereas the stock of certain old-line established companies may trade between $50 and $100 per share. Also, shareholders typically like to trade in round lots, with a round lot usually consisting of 100 shares. The long and short of it is that when the price of a company's stock gets near the top end of its ordinary trading range, a company often will split the stock two for one, or do a 100 percent stock dividend. That will mean twice as many shares will be outstanding. It also will mean, since the company's total value remains the same, that the price of the stock in the market will drop by half, putting the price at the bottom end of its ordinary range. It then will cost a shareholder half as much to buy one round lot of that stock.

What's the other reason for a publicly held company to do a stock split or stock dividend?

Companies sometimes do low percentage stock dividends or stock splits as a shareholder relations device. Unsophisticated investors usually think they are getting something for nothing when they receive a stock certificate in the mail that gives them extra shares of a company's stock as a result of a stock split or stock dividend. Those shareholders have probably not watched the market carefully day by day and therefore do not know that the market has adjusted the price of the corporation's stock to take account of the fact that more shares were outstanding. All that will have happened, of course, is that the same corporate pie will have been cut into smaller pieces.

CHAPTER

9

Getting Information About Companies Invested In

***What information will I be sent by my broker
about companies I have investments in?***

Without being asked to do so, your broker perhaps will
not send you any information about companies whose
securities you own. You would be wise to tell your broker, however, that you wish to see reports put out by the
firm's research department on those companies. Also, if
you own securities in "Street name," you may get
through your brokerage firm materials that the company
itself sends out.

***What materials should I expect to get
from companies I own stock in?***

Each company you own stock in will send you an annual
report in connection with an annual meeting at which

directors are to be elected. Most companies publish these in the spring. These reports contain the company's basic financial statements and other information about the company's operations during the previous year. If you happen to be a photography buff, you will enjoy looking at the photographs that typically fill these reports. Companies generally spare no expense in putting on a good face through their annual reports. You also may receive quarterly reports, but they will be very short and will contain mostly quarterly financial information. Finally, you should expect to receive at least one proxy statement each year, in connection with a corporation's annual meeting. Proxy statements are discussed in the next chapter.

Are other reports available from companies I own stock in?

If you want more information than the annual report and the proxy statement provide, you can obtain a copy of the company's form 10-K annual report filed with the Securities and Exchange Commission. That report, which is filed every March by most companies, contains a fairly detailed description of the company and its activities. If you wish to obtain a copy of that report, you merely need to call the company, ask for the shareholder relations department, and tell them you want a copy of the 10-K.

Is there other information that I can obtain from companies I own stock in?

Companies may publish material designed for consumption by shareholders, and if the company has done so, you can obtain that information through its shareholder relations department. Also, that department will be glad to send you other information it has available about the company, perhaps, for example, brochures about the company's products. In addition, the shareholder relations department can provide you information about recent developments, and probably can provide you copies of press releases the company has issued recently.

What's the best way for me to follow a stock's price?

Many daily newspapers publish complete reports of transactions on the New York and American Stock Exchanges, along with extensive reports on the over-the-counter market. If your local newspaper does not do so, the *Wall Street Journal* and *New York Times* are available in a great many places for daily delivery. With respect to stocks traded on a stock exchange, the reports on stocks will give you the high and low prices for the last fifty-two weeks, along with the amount of the current annual dividend being paid on the stock, if any. You then will be given the volume of trades along with information on the prices at which the stock opened and closed, and the high and low prices for the day. Finally, you will be given the net change in the stock's price during the day. Note that these prices are shown not in dollars and cents, but in dollars and fractions of a dollar. The fraction one-eighth represents 12.5 cents, for example. These reports also show the current ratio of the stock's price to its annual earnings.

CHAPTER

10

Proxy Statements and Proxy Voting

PROXY STATEMENTS

What is a proxy statement?

A proxy statement is a document sent to shareholders in publicly held corporations whenever their votes are solicited in connection with a shareholders' meeting. (And, under federal law, if shareholders' proxies are not solicited in connection with a meeting, the company is required to send them a document containing essentially the same information as a proxy statement, but the document is then called an information statement.) Proxy statements are generally required to be sent by anyone who solicits a proxy in a publicly held corporation, but except in the case of proxy fights, which will be discussed below, it is only the company's management that solicits proxies and therefore sends out proxy statements.

What information do proxy statements contain?

For a garden-variety annual meeting at which the major item to be voted on is the election of directors, the proxy statement will contain mostly basic information about the people the company's management is nominating to be directors, along with detailed information about the compensation that the company pays to its officers and directors, both directly in cash and through such benefits as stock option plans and retirement plans. The proxy statement will also contain information on stock ownership by officers and directors, and by major shareholders. If something special is to be voted on at a shareholders' meeting, such as a merger, the proxy statement will contain information about whatever the shareholders are to vote on.

Who tells management and others what to put in proxy statements?

Under the Securities Exchange Act of 1934, the Securities and Exchange Commission is given broad power to demand that management and others soliciting proxies disclose whatever information the SEC believes important for the protection of investors. The SEC has passed a large number of rules for this purpose.

Why is a company's management required to disclose information about its members' compensation?

The idea behind most of the federal securities laws, including those relating to the proxy system, is, as stated by Justice Brandeis, "Sunshine is said to be the best of disinfectants; electric light the most efficient policeman." Salaries of many corporate officers are startlingly high now. One can only guess how much higher salaries would be if management could pay itself any compensation it wished without having to disclose it. The limit would be that of human greed, and I'm not sure there is any limit to that.

Can shareholders put anything in management's proxy statement if they want to communicate with other shareholders?

Yes. Under the SEC's rule 14a-8, management is required to include in its proxy statement proposals made by security holders, along with limited supporting statements, when certain conditions are met. For annual meetings, the usual rule is that such proposals have to be received by the company at least 120 days in advance of the month and day of the proxy materials used in connection with the previous year's annual meeting. The person submitting a proposal must own, and have owned for at least a year, a minimum of 1 percent or $1,000 in market value of the securities entitled to be voted at the meeting. Very important is the fact that the proposal itself must meet certain requirements or management may exclude it from the proxy statement.

What are grounds for refusing to include a security holder's proposal in management's proxy statement?

Management may refuse to include a proposal on a large number of grounds. One is if the proposal relates to the election of directors. Another is if the proposal deals with a matter relating to the conduct of the ordinary business operations of the company. Yet another is if, under the laws of the corporation's state of incorporation, the proposal is not a proper subject for action by security holders.

What's the best way for a security holder to get a proposal in management's proxy statement?

First, go to the local library and get a copy of rule 14a–8 under the Securities Exchange Act of 1934. Make sure you follow all of its requirements, and avoid the grounds for management's refusing to include the proposal. Actually, most proposals that shareholders want to make would not generally be a proper subject for action by security holders under state corporation law, and therefore management could exclude those proposals from the proxy statement. However, that problem can be avoided by phrasing a proposal as one merely recommending or requesting action by the board of directors.

How often do proxy statements contain proposals by security holders?

In the case of large corporations, they almost always contain shareholder proposals. Some of these proposals relate directly to the monetary interest of shareholders, but many others seem oriented toward changing corporate policy for the benefit of society. For example, in recent years proposals relating to doing business in South Africa have been common.

Do proposals by security holders ever win?

Proposals by shareholders almost never win if they are opposed by management. Management is given the right to put in the proxy statement its own statement either supporting or recommending against any proposal. Most individual investors still follow the so-called Wall Street rule of investors, which is that you should either support management or sell your securities. Most shareholders vote against shareholder proposals that are opposed by management.

Does the fact that security holders' proposals almost always fail to get enough votes to win mean they are not worth doing?

The management of publicly held corporations pay a good deal of attention to the voting on proposals by shareholders. If a proposal receives more votes than management expects, management likely will give serious thought to what it can or should do in response to the proposal. The numbers that might make a difference here are quite small. For example, management might expect a particular proposal to get, say, 4 percent of the vote. If that proposal were to get 8 percent, management would view the vote almost as a revolution.

Do you suggest that shareholders get involved in making these proposals?

No, most shareholders have very little interest in such things, and I do not suggest that that should change. My point is that shareholders should realize the very loud statement they can make by voting in favor of a particular proposal that they agree with. I do, then, think it makes sense to read those proposals and vote on the ones that interest you.

Proxy Voting

What is a proxy?

A proxy is a document that authorizes one or more other people to vote your shares. You will be sent a proxy along with your proxy statement. The proxy will be printed on a fairly small card that can be mailed back in a business size envelope, which will be enclosed along with the proxy. On the proxy you will be asked to appoint a number of different people as your proxy holders, and you will be asked to give any one of them the right not only to vote your shares, but to appoint others as substitute proxy holders. All that is to guard against the problems that would occur if only one or two proxy holders were named in a proxy and they were, for example, sick on the date of the meeting.

On the proxy card you will also be given the opportunity to specify how you want the proxy holders to vote on any of the proposals, either those by management or those by shareholders, that are described in the proxy statement. In the election of directors, you will be given the chance to tell proxy holders either to vote for a candidate or to withhold your vote. (The joke of it is that, under state corporation law, if in a particular corporation new directors could not be elected because they did not get enough votes, the old directors would remain in office. In most corporations, directors tend to be elected year after year, with only a couple of seats changing in any year. What all that means is that if the shareholders refused to elect management's slate of directors most of the same people would still be the corporation's directors anyway.)

Why do corporations go to all the expense and trouble of soliciting proxies?

Under state corporation law, corporations must have annual meetings at which the shareholders elect directors. In large publicly held corporations, share ownership typically is spread very broadly, with no person or institution owning a large percentage of the corporation's shares. Without soliciting proxies, then, most large publicly held corporations could not gather together enough shareholders to constitute a quorum at a meeting.

Who gets to vote stock that is held in "Street name"?

Under federal law, proxy statements and proxies must be passed on to the beneficial owners by the firms and institutions that are the record owners. Corporations and brokerage firms can manage that in more than one way. The important thing from the investor's standpoint is that either the company or your brokerage firm will mail the proxy statements and a proxy to you if you own the corporation's stock in "Street name." Whoever holds the record title to your securities will be required to vote in any way you specify on your proxy.

Proxy Fights

What is a proxy fight?

A proxy fight occurs when competing groups, one of them usually being a corporation's management, engage in an information war trying to get shareholders to sign proxies sent by the group. Proxy fights are not common, partially because they are astronomically expensive (postage alone for one mailing to shareholders may cost several hundred thousand dollars). Proxy fights do occur, however, and they can get very nasty. Typically, the goal in a proxy fight is to take over the management of a company. Legally, the last proxy a shareholder delivers is the proxy that governs, so you can sign one proxy and then later decide to sign another one presented by the other side.

Mergers, Tender Offers, Stock Repurchases and Exchanges

MERGERS

What happens when corporations merge?

In legal terms, when corporations merge, one of them survives and the other or others go out of existence. By law, the surviving corporation takes all the assets and liabilities of the other corporation or corporations that entered into the merger.

How do corporations merge, and what is the role of shareholders?

In most situations, the board of directors of each corporation approves a plan of merger and then submits the plan to the corporation's shareholders for approval. If the shareholders approve, the plan of merger is filed with the proper state official, and then the merger becomes effective in accordance with the plan. If, however, one corporation owns 90 to 95 percent of the stock of another corporation, the law usually allows a merger of the corporations without shareholder approval. If the approval of shareholders is required in a publicly held corporation, the shareholders will be sent a detailed proxy statement containing information about the merger.

What happens to the interest of shareholders in a corporation that is merged out of existence?

The shareholders of a corporation that is merged out of existence receive, as part of the merger, whatever the plan of merger provides. Typically they either receive cash or stock in the surviving corporation. As a practical matter, in most situations, the plan of merger has to give shareholders a good enough deal to get them to approve the merger. Sometimes the deal offered shareholders is not very good, however. This can occur most easily when insiders in a corporation own enough stock to ensure approval of the merger. In that circumstance, insiders may vote for the merger, even if it is not good for the other shareholders, because something in the deal (perhaps something indirect and only related to the merger) is in their interest.

What can investors do if they do not like the deal given them in a plan of merger, besides vote against the plan?

Under the corporation law of most states, shareholders who vote against a plan of merger can ask a court to appraise the value of their shares and then force the surviving corporation to pay them the appraised value of their shares in cash. Along with such an action, or entirely separately, investors may be able to bring a lawsuit under federal or state law challenging the merger or seeking damages. Such actions might be based on a breach of duty owed to investors by the company's officers, directors, and major shareholders. As one alternative, such an action might be based on the fact that all material information that should have been given to shareholders, under federal and perhaps also state law, was not given to them in the proxy materials. Shareholders who believe they have been or are about to be cheated in a merger should talk to a lawyer immediately. Typically in such situations, lawyers can represent not only an individual investor, but all investors who are similarly situated, and typically the legal fees can be paid out of any recovery the lawyers are able to obtain. That means that even a small injury to an individual shareholder can justify the best possible legal representation, because serious money is involved when that injury is multiplied by the others similarly situated. (See chapter 14 for discussions of how to find the right lawyer and of fee arrangements.)

If a plan of merger says that shareholders of one company are to receive in the merger the shares of another company, how does the issuance of the new stock certificates occur?

The surviving corporation will appoint one or more banks to handle the mechanics involved. Typically, about all that will be required is getting the old stock certificates into the hands of the bank, which will issue new certificates against cancellation of the old ones. If an investor holds title to securities in "Street name," the investor's brokerage firm will handle the transaction for the investor.

What happens if a shareholder does not turn in his or her old stock certificate and therefore doesn't get a certificate representing shares in the surviving corporation?

The switch in stock ownership from one corporation to another occurs automatically when the plan of merger becomes effective. The question of stock certificates is just a mechanical one, since stock certificates merely provide evidence of the ownership of stock. The whole thing can be straightened out, even many years after the merger goes through. Occasionally one hears of someone finding in an attic an old stock certificate for a corporation that no longer exists, which after research turns out to represent shares in a corporation that is a successor by merger to the old corporation.

TENDER OFFERS

What is a tender offer?

Neither the Securities and Exchange Commission nor the courts have decided on an exact definition of a tender offer. From the viewpoint of the average investor in the typical tender offer, however, a tender offer looks like this: a company announces publicly that it will buy some or all of the shares of another company's stock in exchange for cash, shares of stock in the offering company, or some combination. The offer to buy will always be at a premium over the current market price of the target company's stock. A 20 percent premium is about the lowest one typically sees, and premiums often go much higher than that. Typically, the offer is made contingent upon the offering company's being able to purchase a set percentage of the target's stock, such as a majority. Typically, also, the offer will be open only for a limited period of time. Investors usually learn about a tender offer from seeing an advertisement, usually a full page, in a newspaper like the *Wall Street Journal* or the *New York Times* or receiving a telephone call from their broker.

What's the difference between a hostile and a friendly tender offer?

In a hostile tender offer, the management of the target company fights the tender offer. Typically this is done both by a publicity campaign, designed to convince shareholders not to tender their shares, and by filing one or more lawsuits alleging legal problems with the tender offer. In a friendly tender offer, the management of the target company goes along with the tender offer rather than fights it.

When a target company's management fights a tender offer that could make a lot of money for the target company's shareholders, can't the shareholders sue management for violating its duty toward shareholders?

Many shareholders have sued management for fighting tender offers, but they have very seldom been successful in winning such lawsuits. If the target company's management is represented by lawyers who know what they are doing, management can usually put up a fight without running a substantial risk of losing a lawsuit brought by shareholders. The right of target company management to fight a tender offer must be based on the management's desire to benefit the corporation, at least in the long run. Also, when it becomes clear that the company will be acquired by means of a tender offer, management has a duty to try to get the best price it can for its shareholders. Management can get in trouble if it continues to fight a losing battle.

Are tender offers regulated by law?

Yes, tender offers are regulated by both federal and state law. The federal legislation, which amended and added a number of sections to the Securities Exchange Act of 1934, is known as the Williams Act. The Williams Act, and the rules under the Williams Act that the Securities and Exchange Commission has passed, contain three types of provisions:

1. Those requiring that various disclosures be made in connection with tender offers;
2. Those making certain provisions a part of all tender offers; and
3. One prohibiting various types of fraudulent conduct in connection with tender offers.

Most of these provisions are only applicable, however, to tender offers for publicly held companies. State regulation of tender offers varies greatly from state to state and generally is not of great concern to the individual shareholder unless the shareholder is considering taking legal action.

What provisions giving rights to shareholders do the Williams Act and its rules make a part of all tender offers for shares of publicly held corporations?

The main provisions of the Williams Act and its rules for the protection of investors in publicly held corporations are the following, which apply in most circumstances:

1. A tender offer must be open to everyone who owns the class of shares the bidder wants to buy;
2. The amount paid to any shareholder must be the highest amount paid to any other shareholder during the tender offer;
3. Any person who tenders shares in response to a tender offer has the right to withdraw those shares at any time while the tender offer is open; and
4. If a tender offer is for less than all of the shares of a particular class, and if more shares are tendered than the bidder wants to buy, the bidder must buy the

shares pro rata from all the shareholders who have tendered their shares.

What happens if a shareholder in a target corporation decides not to accept a tender offer, but the tender offeror acquires most of the other shares in the target corporation?

In that situation, a tender offeror usually will force out of the target corporation any shareholders who did not accept the tender offer. Tender offerors do that by causing the target corporation to merge with another corporation that is owned by the tender offeror. Since the tender offeror at that point will own enough shares in the target corporation to ensure a favorable shareholder vote on the merger, the merger will go through. As a result of the merger, the shareholders in the target corporation will receive in return for their shares whatever the plan of merger provides (with a shareholder typically having a right, under state corporation law, to have a court appraise his or her shares and to receive the payment for the shares in cash, if the shareholder wishes to bring a lawsuit). Very often, the plan of merger provides that shareholders who are forced out receive some debt security of the surviving corporation. In other words, if you decide not to sell, but the tender offer is successful, you probably will not have the option of remaining a shareholder in the target corporation.

What are the real choices an investor has when confronted with a tender offer?

Since tender offers are always made at a significant premium over the current market price, shareholders usually are most concerned about whether they should take the offer or whether there is some other chance for them to get a better deal. It is not unusual for a competing bidder to make a better tender offer while the original tender offer is still open. That sometimes touches off a bidding war that causes the bids to rise in price. Because of the effect of federal law, discussed in a previous answer, a shareholder usually can withdraw shares already tendered to one tender offeror and then tender them to another bidder. Also, the shareholder usually is guaranteed to get the best price paid to any shareholder for shares tendered. So, a shareholder generally can tender shares without fear of missing a better deal later. On the other hand, the shareholder usually can wait and tender at the end of a tender offer period and still be assured of having his or her shares bought pro rata with the shares of those who tendered earlier.

As soon as a tender offer is announced, the price of the shares will rise in the trading market to take account of the bid. Often, the price rises to a level that is near the tender offer price. One choice shareholders need to consider is selling their shares in the market rather than waiting to see what will happen with the tender offer.

Why would shareholders want to sell shares in the market rather than wait to see if the tender offer price may be raised, or if a bidding war may be started by some new bidder?

A shareholder may wish to sell in the trading market to lock in a favorable price. Especially if the tender offer is a hostile one, it may never go through. After a tender offer fizzles, the market price of the target corporation's stock almost certainly will drop immediately. So, a big question is, Do you take your money and run or hold out for a possibly better deal?

This is probably a good point at which to introduce another resident of the investment menagerie: the arbitrageur. Arbs, as they are called, are often on the other side of the transaction when small investors sell in the trading market during a takeover. They are quite well rewarded for taking exactly the risk we have just been discussing.

What is a leveraged buyout?

In a leveraged buyout, often simply called an LBO, a corporation's management, or some outside firm that may or may not have the cooperation of management, takes over a corporation, usually by means of a tender offer, and borrows massively to finance the buyout. Leveraged buyouts were very popular in the 1980s, and most of the borrowing to pay for them was done by issuing junk bonds (which I discussed earlier).

STOCK REPURCHASES AND EXCHANGES

In what circumstances do corporations repurchase their own stock?

Preferred stock is often repurchased for basically the same reason that a corporation likes to pay off its debt, essentially because, from a financial standpoint, preferred stock in a publicly held corporation is considered almost equivalent to debt.

The situation, however, is different with common stock. Sometimes corporations have substantial cash available at a time when management believes that the corporation's common stock is undervalued in the market. In that circumstance, management may cause the corporation to buy back a portion of the outstanding common stock. By decreasing the number of shares outstanding, the proportion of the corporation represented by each outstanding share rises, and that may cause the market price to rise also. (Remember that the corporation has less cash after a repurchase, though, and that goes into the equation also.) Sometimes a corporation's management decides that it would be better for the corporation's common shareholders if the corporation were more highly leveraged. In that situation, the corporation may sell some debt security, such as bonds or debentures, and use the proceeds of the offering to repurchase common stock. After that has been done, the remaining shares of common stock are, then, more highly leveraged.

What is an exchange offer?

In an exchange offer, as the term is used here, a corporation goes to the holders of a particular type of its security, typically preferred stock, and offers to exchange that security for some other security of the corporation. The preferred shareholders may, for example, be offered common stock in exchange for their preferred, or they might be offered preferred stock having different characteristics. Alternatively, they may be offered some debt security in exchange for their preferred stock. The choices here are virtually unlimited.

Are stock repurchases and exchanges regulated by law the way mergers and tender offers are?

Yes, stock repurchases and exchanges are governed by the provisions of both state corporation law and state and federal securities law. These provisions regulate the mechanics that must be followed and also are designed to protect shareholders from unfair or fraudulent conduct.

Limitations on the Resale of Securities (and on Short-Swing and Insider Trading Generally)

Are there any legal limitations on the resale of securities by investors?

Yes, under federal law there are at least four different kinds of limitations on resales. There are further restrictions in state laws. None of these affects the ability of the ordinary investor in usual circumstances to resell securities purchased in the trading market, however.

What are the situations that give rise to legal limitations on resales under federal law?

Federal law places limitations on the resale of securities in at least the following four situations:

1. When an investor owns securities that are restricted securities or that were purchased in an intrastate offering under the Securities Act of 1933;

2. When the investor is an affiliate of the issuer of the securities;

3. When the investor is, under the special conceptions of federal law, an officer, director, or beneficial owner of more than 10 percent of a class of a publicly held company's equity securities; and

4. When the investor is in possession of material inside information.

(The last two situations involve problems with purchases as well as resales.)

RESTRICTED SECURITIES AND SECURITIES PURCHASED IN AN INTRASTATE TRANSACTION

How does an investor end up with restricted securities?

Basically, an investor gets restricted securities if he or she acquired those securities directly or indirectly from the issuer, or from an affiliate of the issuer (or, in certain circumstances, even from a private investor), not in the trading market but in any of a number of types of transactions that are exempt from the registration requirements of the Securities Act of 1933. That is not a technical definition of restricted securities, but it is close enough for our purposes here. (Some of the transactions that give rise to restricted securities were discussed in chapter 5.)

As used in this context, an "affiliate" of an issuer is a person in a control relationship with the issuer. That is, either controlling, controlled by, or under common control with the issuer (affiliates are discussed more below). The certificate for any security that is restricted should bear a legend disclosing that fact, although you cannot rely on that. The long and short of it is that, unless you buy securities in the trading market, in a registered public offering, or in a regulation A or rule 504 or intrastate offering, you should be concerned about whether you are taking restricted securities.

What are the restrictions on resales of restricted securities?

It is possible to sell restricted securities in a private transaction, but you would need a lawyer's help to do that properly. The lawyer would have to make sure the transaction would not violate federal or state law. Depending on the circumstances, that could at least require offering and selling to those who meet certain requirements and who are purchasing for certain purposes. This is very tricky, and it is no place for going it on your own.

What about resales of restricted securities in the trading market?

As a practical matter, you will be required to follow the requirements of rule 144 of the Securities and Exchange Commission for a resale of restricted securities in the trading market (at least if the securities were purchased after early 1972), and the company that issued the securities obviously will have to be publicly held. The rule is complex, and investors usually need the help of lawyers to comply with it.

From an investor's standpoint, the most stringent requirement of rule 144 is a holding period generally of at least two years, with there being lots of details in the rule as to how that period is calculated in various circumstances. There are also other limitations, such as an amount limitation and a requirement that certain information be available to the public about the company, along with the requirement that a form be filed with the SEC in many circumstances.

There are also requirements as to the manner of sale of securities in a rule 144 transaction, those being essentially that the transaction has to be a regular transaction in the trading market. All or almost all of the limitations of the rule, however, are lifted for most nonaffiliates of the issuer when restricted securities have been held at least three years. (Investors who purchase large amounts of securities in private transactions often negotiate registration rights with the company selling the securities. These rights allow the investor to demand that the company register the securities for resale with the SEC and state securities agencies.)

How does an investor go about selling restricted securities under rule 144?

If you hold restricted securities and wish to sell them under rule 144, one way to began is to go to your broker and ask what your brokerage firm will require before selling the securities for you. Many brokerage firms have forms of documents that they want to have completed before they will do a rule 144 transaction. If that does not provide you a helpful starting point, you can immediately call a lawyer for help or you can contact the company and ask the company what it suggests you do to begin the process. Ultimately, you will almost certainly need a lawyer unless the company helps you with the sale, perhaps through one of its lawyers.

What are the limitations on the resale of securities purchased in an intrastate offering?

Basically, securities purchased in an intrastate offering (discussed in chapter 5) will have to be either held by the purchaser, or offered and sold only to persons who could legally have purchased in the intrastate offering, for a minimum period of nine months. (The minimum period can even be one year or more, depending on some technicalities.) If the offering was done properly, everything was spelled out in the documents given to investors, and there should be no mystery in the minds of those who purchased securities about the nature of the transaction and the resale limitations.

How does one sell securities that were purchased in an intrastate transaction, either after or before the holding period has passed?

Any certificate representing securities purchased in an intrastate offering should be legended against transfer. You cannot, however, rely upon that having been done. In any case, when an investor wants to sell those securities after the required holding period has been met, the investor should contact the company and discuss its procedures for allowing resales.

It is possible legally to offer and sell the securities before the holding period has been met, so long as no person who is not a "resident" of the state is involved in the offer or sale. Before attempting such a resale, however, an investor should get good advice from a securities lawyer about what can and can't be done, including who would be considered a "resident" in the particular circumstances. And an investor would also have to get the blessing of the company to do the transaction, since no transfer of the securities could be made without the company's approval.

SECURITIES HELD BY AFFILIATES

What does it take for an investor to be an affiliate of a company that has issued securities?

The question of who is an affiliate is a complex one, depending on many different circumstances. Roughly, however, it can be said that an investor likely is an affiliate of a company if the investor is an officer, director, or substantial shareholder of the company, or sometimes of a related company, such as a parent or subsidiary. The question usually comes down to whether the investor is one of a group of persons who control the company, who participate in controlling the company, or who have at least the power to participate in controlling the company. Regrettably, the concept of "control" is very tricky.

How much stock does an investor need to own before the stock ownership will make the person an affiliate?

Ten percent ownership traditionally has been used as a rule of thumb for determining affiliate status, but there is no way to tell without looking at a particular circumstance, and, frankly, it's not easy to tell for sure in a lot of situations. A shareholder might be an affiliate with less than 10 percent stock ownership, or the investor might not be an affiliate even if he or she owns more than 10 percent of a company's stock.

What resale limitations are there on securities held by affiliates?

As in the case of restricted securities, affiliates can sell securities in private transactions under certain circumstances. They would need the help of a lawyer in doing so, and such transactions carry with them a major problem: the securities in the hands of the new owner would be restricted securities. As a practical matter, affiliates who desire to sell securities of their company in the trading market need to follow rule 144, which was discussed above in connection with restricted securities. One nice thing about the use of rule 144 in the sale of securities owned by affiliates is that so long as the securities are not restricted securities, there is no holding period required. Securities owned by affiliates are traditionally called "control securities."

So, control securities may or may not also be restricted securities?

Yes. The definitions of control and restricted securities are entirely different. Depending on the facts, a security may be a restricted security, a control security, or both. It just depends on whether one or the other or both of the separate definitions are met.

Are all securities owned by affiliates subject to resale limitations?

Yes, it does not matter what securities of a company the affiliate owns or how the affiliate acquired those securities. Any securities owned by an affiliate of a company are control securities, and there are resale limitations on all control securities. For example, say the president of a publicly held company buys 100 shares of the company's common stock on the New York Stock Exchange. The president may not turn around and sell those securities freely on the stock exchange. As indicated, the president can sell them on the exchange, without waiting for a holding period, but the other requirements of rule 144 will have to be met. For example, there will be an amount limitation on the president's resales, certain information must then be publicly available about the company, the securities must be sold in the ordinary way, and a form must generally be filed with the Securities and Exchange Commission giving notice of the resale.

SHORT-SWING TRADING: SECTION 16(B)

What special resale limitation is there on officers and directors of publicly held companies and on people who own more than 10 percent of one of the company's equity securities?

Basically, such people are subject to the so-called short-swing trading provisions of section 16(b) of the Securities Exchange Act of 1934, along with the related requirement to file forms with the SEC under section 16(a). Those provisions, and the rules that go along with them, are complex. It can be very tricky to figure out, for example, who is an "officer" for this purpose and also how beneficial ownership is determined in unusual situations. The situation gets especially complex when one is considering securities like options to purchase stock and securities that are convertible into stock. Some of the most difficult issues arise in connection with various compensation plans, such as stock option and stock purchase plans.

What are the short-swing trading provisions?

Basically, section 16(b) provides that if any profit is made, by a person who is subject to its provisions, on any purchase and sale or sale and purchase of any equity security issued by the person's company, then the profit is to be paid over to the company if the transactions occurred within less than six months of each other.

How are profits calculated for this purpose?

Courts generally figure profits in a way that is designed to squeeze out all possible profits. For example, a director of a company could engage in five purchases and five sales of his or her company's stock during a period of less than six months that, when taken together, netted the director a loss. If, however, it is possible to match a higher sale price with a lower purchase price during the period, a court will say the director had profits for the purposes of section 16(b), and those profits must be paid over to the company. Here's one other trick in calculating profits: each separate transaction is broken down into whatever components are necessary, share by share if that's what it takes, to calculate maximum profits. For example, a purchase on February 1 of 50 shares, and another purchase on November 1 of 50 shares, might be matched against a 100 share sale on July 1. Notice that it is irrelevant that the two dates of purchase are more than six months apart. The only thing that is relevant is that a purchase can be matched with a sale that, in each case, was less than six months apart.

What is the reason for stripping profits away from investors?

Section 16(b) is designed to help minimize the benefits that corporate insiders can get from misusing the inside information they are privy to. It is just a rough rule-of-thumb kind of provision where Congress decided that stopping insiders from getting profits on transactions that are close in time to each other would help prevent some inside information from being misused. The really sad thing about section 16(b) is that, partly because it is so tricky, most people who get into trouble under the section do so by error in transactions that do not involve insider trading.

INSIDER TRADING: RULES 10B-5 AND 14E-3

What is the prohibition on insider trading under rule 10b-5?

Section 10(b) of the Securities Exchange Act of 1934 is an antifraud provision. Rule 10b-5 under section 10(b) is broadly written, but for our purposes here, its main thrust is to prohibit company insiders from purchasing or selling securities when they are in possession of material inside information, and also to prohibit them from providing that information to anyone else for the purpose of trading. Usually, if someone outside a corporation is provided material inside information by an insider, the person outside the corporation is also prohibited from trading. (Technically, one can make proper disclosure of the inside information to the public and then trade, but that rarely is a practical possibility.)

Who is an "insider" for this purpose?

The question of who is an insider sometimes gets tricky, but as a general rule, anyone who works for the company, either directly or indirectly (such as someone who works for an outside firm that does work for the company), will be considered an insider. Also, in general, anyone else who has access to inside information because of his or her position will be considered an insider, and the relationship giving access can be informal. For example, if the chief executive officer of a company were to ask a friend for advice about a company problem, the friend would be considered an insider.

Is it always true that if someone outside the company gets material inside information from an insider, rule 10b-5 prohibits the person outside the company from trading?

No, it all depends on the circumstances. Basically, before one is subject to the trading constraints of rule 10b-5, one has to have some duty that leads to the trading constraint. Typically that would be some relationship, either direct or indirect, formal or informal, with the company. Also, as indicated in a previous answer, the trading constraints usually apply when an insider provides someone outside the company with inside information. For example, if a company officer tells a friend about a company development so the friend can buy the company's stock, the friend is prohibited from trading.

People outside the company are not prohibited from trading, however, if they get information under circumstances where they have no duty with respect to the information. For example, say you're a passenger waiting to board an airliner and you by chance overhear two other passengers discussing a great new product their company has developed, mentioning the company's name. In that circumstance, you have no duty to the company or anyone else that would prevent you from trading on the information. (Note that, if the information related to a planned tender offer, the story would be different because of rule 14e-3, which is discussed at the end of this chapter; note also that state law may vary from rule 10b-5.)

If an insider purposely gives material inside information to someone outside the company, is the person outside the company always prohibited from rading on the information?

No, there is at least one exception, but it's an exception you wouldn't expect to find very often. In a famous case, a former officer of a company told a securities analyst about massive fraud inside the company. The analyst worked hard to see if the story was true and to bring the facts to light. While conducting his investigation, the analyst told customers of his securities firm about the allegations, and those persons traded on the information. Later the Securities and Exchange Commission charged the analyst with violating rule 10b-5. The Supreme Court, however, said that there was no rule 10b-5 violation because the corporate insider breached no duty to his corporation by disclosing the information in the circumstances, because he did it to try to bring the fraud to light. The court also said that since there was no breach of duty by the insider, there could be no breach of duty by the analyst. Note that this was a very unusual case, and you should not expect the kind of thing that got the analyst off to help people in very many circumstances. In virtually all cases, if an insider passes information to an outsider, that outsider will have a duty to refrain from trading or from tipping other people with the information. (Any tippees of the person outside the company also would be subject to the same constraints.)

What does it take for information to be material?

The question of what is material in a given circumstance is often not easy to answer. The basic rule in the context of purchasing or selling a security is that a bit of information is material if there is a substantial likelihood that a reasonable investor would attach importance to the information in determining whether to purchase or sell the security. Note that the issue of whether something is material ends up being looked at by the Securities and Exchange Commission or a court after the fact. This makes it very dangerous for an investor. Remember that there is nothing clearer than 20/20 hindsight.

Is rule 10b-5 the only prohibition on insider trading? What about rule 14e-3?

There are other prohibitions on insider trading besides rule 10b-5, under federal law and state law, and they vary in their prohibitions and effects. Rule 14e-3 under the Securities Exchange Act of 1934 is very important. If someone has taken a substantial step to commence (or has commenced) a tender offer, that rule generally makes it illegal to purchase or sell (or cause to be purchased or sold) securities that are or are to be the subject of a tender offer (or certain related securities) at any time when a person "is in possession of material information relating to such tender offer which information he knows or has reason to know is nonpublic and which he knows or has reason to know has been acquired" from the tender offeror or the target, or from an agent of either. Rule 14e-3 also prohibits tipping other people about information relating to a tender offer. Note that, unlike rule 10b-5, rule 14e-3 is applicable even when you received the inside information under circumstances in which you had no general duty with respect to the information. The information could, for example, have been innocently overheard in a public place.

Part IV

SCAMS, SWINDLES,
FRAUDS, AND
PLAIN MISTAKES
(AND HOW TO
FIGHT BACK)

How many ways are there for investors to be cheated? Let me count the ways. No, I can't count the ways. No one can. There can be as many ways to cheat investors as there are swindlers, con artists, and unscrupulous brokers, and there are lots of each of those. What's more, new ways to cheat investors are being discovered as you read this, and more will be concocted in the future. The current scams, swindles, and frauds that are most often encountered by investors can, however, be grouped into various general types. According to my reckoning, there are ten such groupings, which we'll look at in chapter 13, along with some common mistakes and other problems that may cost you money. The ten scams, swindles, and frauds are:

- straight rip-offs
- pyramid schemes
- misrepresentations and omissions
- insider trading
- unsuitable recommendations
- churning
- unauthorized trading
- excessive mark-ups
- market manipulation
- the misuse of funds and of customers' securities

Chapter 14 then presents ways investors can fight back, including by working through a brokerage firm, the Securities and Exchange Commission, the National Association of Securities Dealers, Inc., and the various stock exchanges. Chapter 14 also covers how a case can be brought to arbitration or a lawsuit filed if necessary, and it discusses how to know when you need a lawyer and how to find the right one.

13

Ways Investors Are Victimized by Mistakes and Are Cheated

COMMON MISTAKES BY BROKERS AND BROKERAGE FIRMS

What are some of the common mistakes by brokers and their firms that cost investors money?

Brokers and brokerage firm clerks often live a helter-skelter existence. That makes it easy for them to make mistakes. Some common mistakes are failing to execute an order, executing an order improperly, not recording a transaction or recording it incorrectly, and misplacing or misdirecting some document or communication. I wouldn't judge a broker or a brokerage firm too harshly just because of a mistake. A mistake once in a while is inevitable. The real problem occurs when the broker or his or her firm fails to take prompt action to set things right. That is what costs investors money. Correcting mistakes should be viewed by brokerage firms simply as the inevitable cost of doing business. Too often, however, they try to avoid their responsibility.

PROBLEMS IN REGISTERED PUBLIC OFFERINGS AND EXEMPT OFFERINGS

What is the biggest problem in registered public offerings and exempt offerings that may cost investors money?

The biggest problem for investors in these offerings is the sale of securities based on materially false or misleading information. The problem can involve fraud, but often the failure to make proper disclosure is caused by mistakes. The reason for the problem is not terribly important, however, as far as the investor is concerned. The securities laws essentially require (at least if those involved in the offering wish to escape liability) that investors be provided with all information that is material in connection with one of these offerings. If securities as sold in a registered or an exempt offering based on material misstatements or omissions, purchasers (often including investors who purchase the securities later, for example, in the trading market) generally have a right to get their money back, or to damages if they no longer own the securities. The same rights accrue to investors who buy in any offering that was made without either registration or a valid exemption from the registration requirements. In all cases, other legal problems may also be involved, which can lead to different remedies being available to an investor. So that a lawyer can appraise the situation later if need be, it is very important that investors keep all written materials given them in offerings and also that they take and keep notes about what was told to them in offerings.

STRAIGHT RIP-OFFS

What is the simplest way investors are cheated?

The simplest scam to work on investors is the straight rip-off. The con artist, who may call himself anything including a broker, causes investors to put money into a nonexistent investment. The so-called investment could purport to be anything from stock in a sure-fire mining venture to pooled certificates of deposit from major banks. Often the promise is of large gains with low risk, but it can be the hope of phenomenal gains with high risk.

How do straight rip-offs usually play out?

Sometimes the people running the scam simply collect all the money they think they can and then disappear. Other times they boldly explain to investors how the deal blew up for some unexpected reason, and then they stay in town to work on their next scam. One explanation that may be given is that the company that was to pay off on the investment suddenly went bankrupt. Those dealing with the investors may show great concern and may tell a convincing story about how they never expected the bankruptcy, or whatever else supposedly caused the scheme to falter.

Are the people investors deal with in straight rip-offs always crooks?

No, and that's one of the most insidious things about these schemes. Really smart con artist don't try to con investors. Rather, they con honest but usually unsophisticated people into fronting for them without knowing it. As a result, the investor in one of these scams may be dealing with someone who is well known and respected in the investor's eyes. When the "investment" finally is seen by the investor as coming to naught, the explanations and obvious distress of the person the investor dealt with may even blind the investor to the fact that the "investment" was a complete fraud rather than merely a business venture gone sour.

PYRAMID SCHEMES

What is a pyramid scheme?

A pyramid scheme works on the same principle as a chain letter. The first persons in the scheme get money from people they bring in, who are suppose to recruit others into the scheme to pay money to others higher up in the scheme, and so on over and over again. In the typical such scheme, investors pay a certain fee for the right to deal in some product. One example is cosmetics to be sold by the dealers directly to the public. What separates this type of pyramid scheme from the entirely legal and sensible franchise is that the real focus of the scheme is not selling products to the public. Rather, the real focus is encouraging the dealers to become "distributors" by bringing in new dealers, and then encouraging the distributors to become higher-level distributors by bringing in new distributors, and so on. At each step in the pyramid, those who bring in new investors, or who talk investors into moving up the pyramid, typically share with the promoters of the scheme any fees paid by dealers and distributors, and also typically they get a cut of the wholesale profits on any products that are sold to the public.

How can I tell the difference between a pyramid scheme and a legitimate franchise?

Sometimes it's not easy. There are franchises that are just barely on the legal side of the line separating pyramid schemes from franchises, and there are pyramid schemes that at first glance look like franchises. Perhaps the biggest thing that distinguishes franchises is that those behind the franchise operation stress the sale of products or services. They focus on bringing into the business people who will buy a franchise and then make their money by working the franchise. Some legitimate franchises do offer investors the opportunity of buying in at a higher level than mere retail dealer, but that's the best way the franchising company sees to work a distribution system for selling the company's products or services. In the pyramid scheme, most of the focus is on making money through bringing in more suckers, not on selling anything.

Can pyramid schemes make money for investors?

Yes, just as in a chain letter, the first investors into a scheme can make money. However, that doesn't last long or include many investors. Very soon the scheme runs out of new investors who can be brought in, and the whole thing falls. Since the real design of the scheme is to bring in investors rather than to sell products or services, the scheme could never ultimately work as a business venture.

What if an investor has a chance to get in early on a pyramid scheme?

First, most investors who knew they were involved in a pyramid scheme couldn't make any money even if they were some of the first people in the scheme. The scheme works for a time because the promoters are consummate con men who so excite people with the prospect of making easy money that the "investors" are happy to share the opportunity with their friends. If you knew it was a scam, you probably couldn't do a very good job of bringing in your friends. And, even if you could, you'd be breaking the law right along with the promoters. In fact, a lot of people involved in pyramid schemes are breaking the law, even if they don't know it.

What is a Ponzi scheme?

A Ponzi scheme is just one version of a pyramid scheme. Ponzi was a con man who lived in Massachusetts. He convinced a lot of people that he was a financial genius because he not only promised investors high returns on their money, he delivered. The scheme went on for some time, and Ponzi took in more and more money. Some of the money he pocketed and some he gave to earlier investors as returns on their money. His scheme was the simplest form of a pyramid scheme, and it differs from a straight rip-off in that money from succeeding investors was used to keep the scam going by paying off earlier investors. Though Ponzi's scheme lasted quite a while, his fraud finally came to light and he went to prison. After prison, he was deported to Italy as an undesirable alien. Mussolini ruled Italy at the time, and he thought Ponzi had been a victim of American prejudice against Italians. Mussolini accepted him as a financial genius and gave him a job in the Italian treasury. When last seen, Ponzi was headed for South America with a bundle of Mussolini's money.

MISREPRESENTATIONS AND OMISSIONS

Misrepresentations by Brokers

What's the biggest problem investors have with brokers who act illegally or unethically?

Unquestionably, misrepresentations of one type or the other, along with the omission to disclose information that should be disclosed, is the most common type of misbehavior by brokers. The problem goes all the way from relatively minor overstatements of a stock's potential to outrageous claims of profitability for companies that exist only as mere shells. Investors need to realize that brokers are basically engaged in selling, and should expect them to exude optimism. However, good brokers tell the truth, and that means the whole truth, and good brokers also push only securities that they honestly believe in. When brokers do otherwise, they violate their customers' trust and, usually, the law.

What are some of the more common ways in which brokers engage in misrepresentation?

Perhaps the most common misrepresentation is as to a stock's likely performance. No one knows what a stock's price will be in the future. Anyone who could predict that with regularity could soon be the richest person in the world. Along with representations go omissions to state facts that are necessary to evaluate the positive things a broker tells investors about a stock. A common omission is the failure to disclose the risks involved in a particular investment.

Beyond those kinds of problems with misrepresentations and omissions, what does an investor particularly have to look out for in this area?

One particularly egregious problem is the operation of boiler rooms. Another is the misrepresentation found in connection with the sale of penny stocks.

Boiler Rooms

What is a boiler room?

A boiler room is the securities industry's equivalent of a den of thieves, all huddled together and talking on telephones to prospective victims. The company they work for will at least call itself a brokerage house, in most circumstances. And the people on the phone may even be authentic brokers, although that's optional. The idea here is to sell largely worthless securities by any means necessary. Sometimes these scams are quite sophisticated, and may be dragged out over a number of weeks. The first couple of phone calls may be just to get acquainted. The "broker" may mention a security and not push it, and then later tell the intended victim how high that stock's price has gone in the meantime. Generally, unsophisticated investors are the most likely victims of boiler rooms, but even savvy investors are taken in by some of the more carefully crafted operations.

Penny Stocks

What is the situation with penny stocks?

There have been so many problems in the penny stock area that Congress and the Securities and Exchange Commission stepped in with special laws and regulations. All too often, brokers selling penny stocks hype them shamelessly regardless of the truth.

Disclosure Problems with Companies

How do misrepresentations and omissions by companies cost investors money?

Publicly held companies are required to disclose a lot of information to the public, which they do on an almost continual basis. When that information is materially incorrect or incomplete, or when the company fails to update information when required, investors who are trading in the public markets buy and sell the company's securities for prices that do not reflect the company's real situation. They may lose money, in other words, because they pay too much when they buy or receive too little when they sell. If the company's failure to make proper disclosure is willful, or if the company acts recklessly, the company commits securities law fraud. Investors may have a right to be paid damages in those circumstances.

INSIDER TRADING

How are investors cheated by insider trading?

When company insiders, or their tippees, buy or sell on inside information, they cheat others trading in the market in the same sort of way card sharks cheat their victims. They have an ace up their sleeve they don't let the other players see. Under the securities laws, people who trade in the markets contemporaneously with inside traders have a right to collect damages. To do that, it's not necessary for an investor to show that he or she actually sold to or bought from an inside trader.

UNSUITABLE RECOMMENDATIONS

Does a broker have a duty to make only suitable recommendations?

Yes, absolutely. Under the rules governing brokers' conduct, brokers are not to make recommendations until they have collected information about the investor's financial situation, investment experience, and investment objectives. After having that information in hand, a broker may not recommend a security without a reasonable ground for believing that the security is suitable for the investor.

Is the recommendation of unsuitable securities a big problem? After all, isn't it in the interest of brokers to recommend the securities that their customers should want?

With some brokers, unsuitable recommendations are a very big problem. Often, for example, an investor's situation calls for putting together a portfolio of stable, safe securities and then pretty much leaving the portfolio alone. The problem with that, from a broker's standpoint, is that after the initial purchases, there is little to be gained from having the account. Brokers who are not entirely scrupulous often find it hard to resist making trading recommendations far more often than necessary in such an account.

Do unsuitable recommendations get made based on pressure from brokerage firms to push certain securities?

No reputable brokerage firm would do that overtly, but brokers are often encouraged by their firms to try to sell certain securities. That might occur, for example, when the firm is underwriting a new issue of securities by some company. In that circumstance and in other circumstances, one way brokers are "pressured" into selling certain securities is by giving them a higher commission than they would get on most transactions. Encouragement to sell certain securities can push brokers toward unsuitable recommendations.

"CHURNING"

What is churning?

Churning is trading for a customer's account for the purpose of generating commissions for the broker rather than profits for the customer.

Does churning occur only in discretionary accounts where a broker has the power to trade for a customer?

No, although churning certainly can most easily be done in a discretionary account. One of the factors courts and arbitrators look for in cases involving churning of non-discretionary accounts is whether the broker in fact exercised control over trading in the account. Courts or arbitrators will look at the situation and try to decide whether or not the customer was in fact able to evaluate the recommendations made by the broker and whether, in light of all the circumstances, the broker in fact controlled the situation.

What has to be shown in order to prove churning?

In addition to control over trading in the account by the broker, an investor generally has to prove that the trading in the account was excessive in light of the investor's investment objectives, and that the broker acted with intent to defraud or recklessly disregarded the client's interests in managing the account.

How can one show that trading in an account is excessive? Isn't that a matter of opinion?

People can disagree over the question of how much trading is too much, although I believe that any trading that is for the purpose of generating commissions rather than profit for the investor is churning. What it comes down to, I believe, is how much trading a court or an arbitrator would want to see to be convinced of the churning. Over the years some ways of looking at trades, and some rules of thumb, have been developed to help recognize churning. These include the turnover rate, the presence of in-and-out trading, and the ratio between the size of the account and the amount of the broker's annual commissions.

What turnover rate indicates churning?

A turnover of securities in an account in excess of six times annually is generally viewed as indicative of churning. An investor must remember, however, that this is just a rule of thumb. In some kinds of accounts, for example an account made up of shares in mutual funds, a much lower annual turnover rate than six would certainly indicate churning, since it generally makes no sense to trade the shares of mutual funds to any extent at all.

What is in-and-out trading?

In-and-out trading refers to the classic trading pattern in churning, where the account is rarely left alone for any long period. Rather, securities in the account are sold and then new ones purchased, followed by more sales and more purchases, and then more of the same over and over.

What ratio between the size of the account and the broker's annual commissions leads one to believe that churning has occurred?

There is no exact number to use here, as the amount of commissions a broker would reasonably earn would vary with the investment objectives of various kinds of customers. The secret here, then, is to compare the annual commissions of a suspect broker with those of brokers in charge of accounts for the same types of customers. When looked at in that way, an excessive commission ratio usually isn't hard to spot.

How much churning goes on?

Since I believe that any trading whatsoever that is for the purpose of generating commissions for a broker constitutes churning, it goes on every day in brokerage firms all over the country. Mostly, customers do not even suspect that their account is being churned. The question of churning tends to come up after a customer has lost a substantial amount of money. If a customer makes money, or at least does not lose much, the customer is not likely to suspect something is wrong. To protect themselves, investors really need to keep their eyes open for excessive trading recommendations.

UNAUTHORIZED TRADING

How do problems with unauthorized trading by brokers typically come up?

Unauthorized trading typically occurs in a couple of different circumstances. First, a broker may buy or sell securities for a client when the broker cannot reach the client and when the broker feels sure what the client would want done. This, of course, can be to the customer's benefit, and if the customer believes that, he or she likely will not complain about an unauthorized trade. In some situations, however, brokers who are overbearing may make an unauthorized trade or two to see what they can get away with, and then accelerate their unauthorized trading to create what is, in effect, a discretionary account.

What should investors especially look out for in terms of unauthorized trading?

I believe investors should be especially wary when they get the first indication that a broker has made an unauthorized trade. If it looks as if the broker acted in the investor's interest in an emergency situation, that is one thing. If it looks as if the broker is trying to test the waters to see how far he or she can go before the investor will speak up, it's time to get a new broker.

EXCESSIVE MARK-UPS

What are mark-ups?

Mark-ups occur only in the over-the-counter market, where brokerage firms make markets in certain securities by buying and selling them for their own account. A mark-up is the amount a market maker adds on for the sale of a security over the price the market maker is paying for the security in the market.

What does it mean for a mark-up to be excessive?

If a number of securities firms make a market in a particular security, the broker is supposed to make the best deal available for a customer. The brokerage firm cannot simply sell the security out of its own inventory at a higher price. If it does so, that's an excessive mark-up. The biggest problem occurs when only one securities firm makes a market in a particular security. In that case, the rules under which securities firms operate require that the mark-up be reasonable. In this regard, the National Association of Securities Dealers, Inc. uses 5 percent as a rule of thumb for looking at mark-ups. Mark-ups that are higher than that have to be looked at closely to see if they are excessive. That does not mean, of course, that a mark-up of 5 percent or less is necessarily reasonable. It would all depend on the circumstances.

In what circumstances do investors need to be particularly on the lookout for an excessive mark-up?

An investor has to be especially suspicious about the possibility of excessive mark-ups anytime the investor's securities firm is the only one that makes a market in a security. When that is the case, the securities firm is required to disclose that fact to the customer, although that disclosure may be in some not very prominent language contained on a confirmation slip.

How often is an investor likely to buy from a sole market maker?

Much more often than would appear likely at first glance. It is, of course, very common for customers to buy the securities that have been recommended to them by their brokers, and in situations where a firm is a security's sole market maker, that firm may well encourage its brokers to recommend that security. There is not, of course, anything necessarily wrong with that. It is just a situation that should put an investor especially on guard.

Is the sole-market-maker situation likely to be found in any particular kind of security?

Yes, that situation is found more often in the penny stock area than in any other. Regrettably, in the penny stock area the fact of being a sole market maker is too often combined with such activities as misrepresentations and omissions and market manipulation.

MARKET MANIPULATION

What is market manipulation?

Market manipulation is essentially anything done to increase or decrease the price of a security artificially. Often it is accomplished by the trading or apparent trading of securities for the purpose of affecting the market price. All sorts of schemes have been devised to manipulate the market price of securities. Prior to the federal securities laws that were passed in the New Deal, there were a number of celebrated cases of large-scale market manipulation, along with a great deal of garden-variety manipulation that occurred on a continuing basis. With tough laws to protect against it, and with the Securities and Exchange Commission and the self-regulatory organizations on the lookout, market manipulation is now not widespread. It does, however, continue to be a problem.

Is market manipulation more likely in one kind of market than in another?

Yes, market manipulation is much more likely in the over-the-counter market than it is on a stock exchange. The nature of the over-the-counter market, with sometimes one or a very few firms making a market in a particular security, is much more conducive to manipulation than is the auction market that exists on exchanges. Also, of course, the total market for a given security tends to be much smaller in the over-the-counter market than on an exchange. It would be difficult, and extraordinarily expensive, to manipulate the market for the stock of a large New York Stock Exchange company, because there is so much of it trading in the market.

What are some of the ways the market price for a security is manipulated?

One way is by putting out false information about the company that issued the security. Other common ways that a market price is manipulated are scalping, wash sales, matched sales, daisy chains, and tie-in sales.

What is scalping?

In a scalping scheme, a brokerage firm itself buys securities in a relatively small company whose stock is traded in the over-the-counter market. Then the firm has its brokers recommend the purchase of that same security to a large number of customers. As those customers purchase the securities, the market price will be driven up by the artificially created demand. The brokerage firm then sells its securities at a profit and stands on the sidelines watching the market price decline after the artificially created demand has stopped.

What is a wash sale?

In a wash sale, a person or firm purchases and sells the same securities at the same time through the same brokerage firm. What that does is create apparent activity in the trading of the stock, which has a tendency to drive up the price of the stock in the market.

What is a matched order?

A matched order is essentially the same as a wash sale, except the purchases and sales are through different brokerage firms. Again, the idea is to create apparent trading activity at prices essentially set by the trader. Obviously, in the case of both wash sales and matched orders, a brokerage firm is in the position to do them most easily.

What is a daisy chain?

In a daisy chain, someone, typically with the connivance of a market maker, engages in a series of trades in a security at successively higher or lower prices. The idea is to drive the price of the security up or down, whichever fits best into the market manipulator's scheme.

What is a tie-in sale?

Tie-in sales occur most often in registered public offerings. In this scheme, a brokerage firm requires someone purchasing securities in a public offering to agree subsequently to purchase additional securities, at a higher price, in the trading market.

When does an investor have to be most on the lookout for market manipulation?

As in so many cases, the penny stock area is the one to watch out for most. Especially when a security has only one market maker, it is easy for that market maker to manipulate the market at will. The opportunity for such manipulation is found more often in the penny stock area than in the ordinary market for over-the-counter securities.

MISUSE OF FUNDS AND CUSTOMERS' SECURITIES

Since brokerage firms typically hold both cash and securities for their customers, do customers have to worry about the misuse of those funds or securities?

The misuse of funds and customers' securities by brokerage firms, or more usually by some unscrupulous broker or other employee of the firm, is not unheard of. Such schemes are not common, however. Also, all reputable brokerage firms carry insurance against losses to customers resulting from the misuse of their funds or securities by brokerage firm employees.

CHAPTER

14

Fighting Back

What can I do if I feel cheated in an investment or victimized by a mistake?

I believe that what I call a stepped response is usually best. That means you start at the lowest step and go to successively higher steps if necessary to get your money back. Do not delay. It is important that you pursue a complaint right away. If you delay, your complaint is not so likely to be taken seriously, and the facts will start to get stale. Also, there are legal limits, set by statutes of limitations and arbitration rules, on how long you have to take legal action or seek arbitration. No matter what else you are doing about your problem, I wouldn't wait more than three or four months from the first questionable event that occurred before speaking with a lawyer. Usually, you should talk to a lawyer much sooner than that.

Where should I start if I'm going to try to get my money back?

Where you start depends, of course, on what kind of problem you have and who caused it. Assuming it's a problem created by your broker, I generally would start with the broker or the branch manager, either on your own or after having talked to a lawyer.

LAWYERS

Should I talk to a lawyer before making a complaint to anyone?

The more money that is involved and the more complicated the situation, the more important it likely will be to talk to a lawyer as early as possible. Frankly, unless you really are sure you don't need to talk to a lawyer before taking some initial action, and you are willing to run the risk that your appraisal of the situation is wrong, I'd suggest you talk to one. If the situation is one where you think it makes sense, for example, to write a letter to a broker or a branch manager, you want your letter to be as effective as possible, and a lawyer can help you with that. If your complaint is not resolved through your efforts, at some point you are going to need to talk to a lawyer anyway if you want to pursue relief, and you may find that a lawyer does not even charge you for discussing your complaint letter and giving you some advice about how to proceed. Often, a lawyer will be happy to help in those ways free of charge, with the idea that you probably will hire the lawyer if you can't get the problem solved yourself. (If yours is the kind of matter that involves a number of other people who have been cheated or victimized in some way, I'd definitely suggest talking to a lawyer before you do anything else, no matter what.) The section below headed "Lawsuits" has a further discussion of lawyers and information on fee options.

How do I find a lawyer to help me?

Finding a lawyer to help with securities problems is a difficult matter. You would like to find a lawyer who is experienced in securities matters and, in most cities, there are not many of those. Unless you have an idea of your own, or unless a friend or business colleague can give you a recommendation, your best bet may be to call a lawyer you have faith in and ask for a recommendation. You may have to hire a lawyer outside your locality to get the right one. So much legal work is conducted by telephone, fax, and overnight delivery services these days that the location of the lawyer isn't as important as you might think at first. But getting the right lawyer is very important.

What should I look for in a lawyer besides experience in securities matters and competence?

In your first contact with a lawyer, which may well be by telephone, focus on how the lawyer treats you and try to decide how you think the lawyer will treat you in the future. Does the lawyer take the time really to listen to you, to hear fully what you are saying? Many don't. Many merely want to rush ahead, probing for answers to the questions *they* think are important. Is the lawyer the kind of person who will be available by telephone, who will return your calls promptly? Sadly, many aren't reachable by telephone, and many will hardly return any calls at all. This has become a big problem in the profession. Are you important to the lawyer? If you don't seem important to the lawyer in an initial contact, you can be sure you won't seem any more important later. Good lawyers consider every client important, and that comes through in a conversation.

BROKERS AND BRANCH MANAGERS

Assuming my problem is with my brokerage firm and I want to proceed on my own, how do I decide whether to go to my broker or to the branch manager?

One question to ask yourself is, Do I want anything more to do with this broker? If so, it usually would make sense to discuss your problem with the broker. Also, you probably will want to go to the broker if you think the problem is one he or she could take care of on his or her own. Finally, you might want to go directly to the broker if you think the broker might help talk the branch manager into making things right with you.

If I decide to complain to the branch manager, what's the best way to do that?

The best way would depend somewhat on the situation and also on your personality and that of the branch manager. One thing you have to ask yourself is whether you can be more persuasive in person or in writing. Often the best approach is a combination of an oral and a written response. For example, you might call and briefly describe your complaint to the branch manager and then suggest that you send him or her the details in writing. In the letter you should carefully describe what happened and explain what you think is wrong. In many cases you also should include copies of any relevant records or documents. In the letter you might also suggest that you would like to come and see the branch manager to discuss the problem. Then, a few days after sending the letter, you could call and set up an appointment to see the branch manager.

How likely am I to have my problem solved by a branch manager?

That depends in large degree on the personality of the manager, as well as, of course, on the strength of your claim and on whether the manager has the authority to resolve claims of your type and size. Even if the manager does not have authority to resolve your problem on his or her own, however, the manager may be able to take your claim up with his or her superiors. That is probably most likely in situations where a broker has done something clearly egregious and the branch manager has already taken the actions within his or her power, such as firing the broker.

BROKERAGE FIRM COMPLIANCE OFFICERS

What should I do next if I can't resolve my complaint with the branch manager?

A sensible next step typically would be contacting the brokerage firm's compliance officer. You can do that by calling the headquarters of the brokerage firm and asking for the compliance office. You then can simply ask to whom you should address a complaint. Your letter to the compliance officer can be essentially the same one you sent to the branch manager, except that you need to add the steps you already have taken to resolve the complaint. You also may want to modify the letter based on things you have learned from dealing with the branch manager.

Are compliance officers really interested in resolving complaints?

Compliance officers typically are serious about trying to prevent wrongdoing or mistakes by brokers, but they may or may not be interested in solving past mistakes that cost the firm money. I regret to say that, in my experience, brokerage firms often will not pay money to satisfy a complaint, almost no matter how valid the complaint, without being forced to.

SECURITIES AND EXCHANGE COMMISSION

What do you suggest my next step be after striking out with the compliance officer?

The first place I'd suggest you go is the Securities and Exchange Commission. A good way to proceed is to call the Commission in Washington and speak with the Office of Consumer Affairs. You can reach that office at (202) 272-7440. Find out from that office the address of the regional office that serves your area. Then send a letter to the regional office detailing your complaint.

What can the Securities and Exchange Commission do?

The SEC takes complaints seriously. What it likely will do is send a copy of your letter to your brokerage firm and ask the firm for an explanation. If whoever gets the SEC's letter finds, after an investigation, that the firm may be in trouble with the SEC, you may find that the firm is suddenly interested in taking care of your complaint in the hope that the SEC will let the matter drop. If the SEC is not satisfied with the firm's explanation, it may open a formal investigation that could lead to sanctions against the firm and persons in the firm. The SEC cannot take direct action to get money for you, however.

SELF-REGULATORY ORGANIZATIONS

Should I limit my complaint at this point to the Securities and Exchange Commission?

Certainly you can wait to see what happens as a result of your complaint to the SEC. However, if nothing comes of that you may have wasted quite a bit of time. I would suggest, therefore, that you also complain to one or more of the self-regulatory organizations. If the problem you complain of relates to something other than problems specifically with transactions on a stock exchange, you can complain to the National Association of Securities Dealers, Inc. You can reach the NASD at 1735 K Street, N.W., Washington, DC 20006. The telephone number is (301) 590-6500. You probably can speed the process along by calling the NASD and asking whether your complaint should be sent directly by you to one of their district offices. If so, they can give you the address of the office nearest you. If you wish to receive from the NASD disciplinary and other information relating to problems including its members, or a broker, you can request that information by calling (800) 289-9999. Information will be mailed to you. If your problem relates to a New York Stock Exchange member firm, you can complain to the New York Stock Exchange, Inc. at 11 Wall Street, New York, NY 10005. You may reach the NYSE by telephone at (212) 656-3000. If something you complain about involves a member of one of the other exchanges, you can, of course, complain to that exchange.

What will self-regulatory organizations do in response to an investor's complaint?

The self-regulatory organizations are likely to handle the complaint in much the same way the SEC does. That is, they will send a letter to the brokerage firm asking for a response to your complaint. Probably, they will send a copy of your letter to the brokerage firm.

What result am I likely to get from complaints to self-regulatory organizations?

The fact that multiple inquiries reach the brokerage firm should increase the concern of the firm that one of the organizations you complain to will take action because of the complaint. This, I believe, increases the chance that the firm will try to make things right with you.

STATE SECURITIES ADMINISTRATORS

Should an investor also make a complaint to a state securities administrator?

Yes. All states have an office that handles securities matters. An investor may have to do a little searching to reach the office, because it's difficult to predict exactly what it may be called in a particular state. (One way to get the address and telephone number of the office in your state is to call the North American Securities Administrators Association at [202] 737-0900.) In some states, an investor's best hope for action comes from the office of the state's securities administrator, but in other states the office will be so understaffed that it will not be able to provide much help. It's worth a try, however.

What control do states securities administrators have over brokerage firms?

It varies by state, but brokers and dealers have to be registered to do business in a particular state, and the state will have a variety of laws and regulations designed to protect investors, including those that provide for sanctions against brokerage firms.

U.S. ATTORNEYS AND LOCAL PROSECUTORS

Should an investor also make a complaint with the U.S. Attorney's Office or the office of the local prosecutor?

If what you are complaining about involves criminal conduct, you may want to complain to the U.S. Attorney's Office or the office of the local prosecutor. However, those offices may want to wait to see what happens with investigations that may be done by the federal or state securities officials. Not infrequently, criminal actions in the securities area are brought after the federal or state securities commission has suggested criminal prosecution to the federal or state prosecutor. Probably the best reason to contact a prosecutor is if you want to pursue the question of prosecution as a matter of seeing justice done.

LAWSUITS

If everything to this point has failed, is the investor's option a lawsuit?

A lawsuit may or may not be an option at this point. For several years, most brokerage firms have put a clause in some or all of their client agreements that requires arbitration and waives the right to sue in court in the case of at least most disputes between the firm and the customer. Especially if an investor is operating under a client agreement signed since the late 1980s (when the U.S. Supreme Court said such arbitration clauses were enforceable), arbitration may be the only remedy. Techniques for dealing with the arbitration clause are suggested in chapter 3

Is it important whether a lawsuit is an available remedy?

Often, arbitration is the best way to proceed, but sometimes it is not. Also, it is almost always better to have available the possibility of a lawsuit. Brokerage firms do not like lawsuits, and usually would much rather face arbitration. Lawsuits are expensive in most cases, so unless a lot of money is involved they often aren't practical. However, sometimes a small claims court can do a nice job with a claim that is small enough to be tried there and simple enough to be handled in the kind of summary proceeding usually found in small claims courts. Arbitrations are conducted in only some cities in the country. If you do not live in one of those cities, you may find that a lawsuit is a reasonable economic alternative, since a lawsuit can be tried where you live. Here, too, it must be remembered that only a small percentage of lawsuits end up in trials. Usually, they are settled along the way. That means that the expense of the trial itself usually is avoided.

How much money has to be involved before a lawsuit is a reasonable alternative?

There is no particular dollar amount that can be given. As indicated above, sometimes a claim can even be handled in a small claims court for a modest cost. One determining factor, in deciding whether a lawsuit is economically feasible, is the complexity of the case. If the facts are straightforward and proving them would be simple from documents, for example, the case should not be very expensive to pursue. However, if the facts are complex and proving them would difficult, that could increase the cost of the lawsuit tenfold.

Is there any way I can avoid paying legal fees out of my own pocket?

Yes. Sometimes lawyers will agree to take a so-called contingent fee. That is, they will agree to be paid out of any money they collect for an investor in a lawsuit.

If a lawyer agrees to take a contingent fee, how can I tell how much the fee will be?

Lawyers always have their clients sign a contingent fee agreement at the beginning of a case. Contingent fees are set as percentages of what the lawyer gets you as a result of negotiations or at the conclusion of an arbitration or a legal action. The percentages vary. A rate of $33\frac{1}{3}$ percent is usual, but the percentage can be lower in some situations. In rare circumstances the percentages can be higher than $33\frac{1}{3}$ percent. In class actions, the legal fees are approved by the court.

Aren't those fee percentages rather steep?

As a lawyer, I may be disqualified from answering that one. I realize that contingent fees sometimes seem steep. But sometimes lawyers spend large amounts of time and great effort, spread over months or years, and end up with nothing. As clients watch their lawyer work on their case, most are relieved, I think, not to have to worry about the legal fees that they know would be mounting quickly if the fee were not contingent.

What determines whether I have a case that a lawyer will take for a contingent fee?

The ethical rules that govern lawyers come into play here, as do economics and other considerations of individual lawyers. What I'd do if I were you is this: if you are interested in discussing having a lawyer take your case for a contingent fee, talk to the lawyer you'd like to have handle the matter, describe your problem, and ask about a contingent fee. That almost never will cost you anything. If the lawyer doesn't want to take the case on the basis of a contingent fee, I'd then ask if the lawyer believes yours is the kind of case in which a contingent fee would be a real possibility with another lawyer. If your case can be brought as a class action, it is almost certain that a lawyer will take a contingent fee.

What is a class action?

A class action is a lawsuit that is brought not only on behalf of the named plaintiff, but on behalf of everyone else similarly situated. Who those people are does not even have to be known initially. In most situations, you probably can figure out for yourself fairly well whether you have a case that might be brought as a class action. Since large amounts of money can easily be involved in class actions even where each investor in the class is out only a small amount of money, lawyers can afford to do a lot of legal work in such actions because of the possibility they will get a substantial fee.

How do I decide whether I should talk to a lawyer about a possible claim?

The best idea is to talk to a lawyer if you think you may have a claim. Since lawyers rarely charge clients for evaluating claims, it is foolish to forgo a claim because you fear that pursuing it may be too expensive. You may find that pursuing it costs you nothing.

ARBITRATION

If I want to go, or have to go, to arbitration, what does that involve?

Most securities arbitrations are handled by the National Association of Securities Dealers, Inc., the New York Stock Exchange, Inc., the American Stock Exchange, Inc., or the American Arbitration Association. The way an arbitration is conducted depends, among other things, on the amount of money involved. For claims of only a few thousand dollars, an investor can have a matter arbitrated purely on documents submitted to a sole arbitrator. That, obviously, is the cheapest way to go. It may well not be the best way, however, since an investor loses the opportunity to appear in person. Appearing in person is something you want, if it makes economic sense, since an investor, or more likely the investor's lawyer, can get a feeling from an arbitrator's questions for what arguments are likely to be most effective.

Where are arbitrations held?

Arbitrations typically are held in only some cities around the country. The availability of the most convenient location may play a major role in choosing the group before which one would present the arbitration.

How much will an arbitration cost?

For the simplest matters, the arbitration fees are typically $150 or less. The arbitration fees go up from there, but rarely would they be more than several hundred dollars. The bigger expense, of course, may be the fee to your lawyer.

How much are we talking about in terms of a lawyer's fee in arbitrations?

If you are involved in the simplest form of arbitration, which does not involve a hearing, a lawyer would charge you very little for looking over your draft of a submission and then making some comments. You may be able to get some very good advice that way for no more than $100 to $200. In some instances a lawyer wouldn't even charge you for that. For a lawyer to prepare your submission, or make substantial changes in your own draft, would cost at least several hundred dollars. For a lawyer to prepare for an arbitration that requires a hearing, one quickly gets into the thousands of dollars. Good lawyers usually discuss with their clients how far the client wants the lawyer to go in preparing a case. If only $20,000 is involved in a matter, it obviously doesn't make sense to spend anything like $20,000 trying to win the case. The best thing to do is have a frank discussion with a good lawyer about how to proceed. A good lawyer will be able to give you a reasonable estimate of what would be involved in pursuing a particular arbitration. Sometimes a contingent fee arrangement will be possible. If so, you won't have to pay anything out of your pocket for a lawyer.

How does an investor begin an arbitration against a brokerage firm?

One thing to do is look at the client agreement you have with your brokerage firm. It may include procedures for beginning an arbitration. Sometimes you can start the process by telling the brokerage firm that you want to go to arbitration. The firm then will set the wheels in motion, including perhaps giving you, say, five days to choose the group you want to handle the arbitration. If you don't choose, the firm may then be able to choose by itself, and you can be sure it will choose the group it thinks will be best for the firm — perhaps because the arbitration group it chooses will conduct the arbitration in some far-off city that is inconvenient for you.

If arbitration procedures aren't covered in the client agreement, or in some other agreement you have with the brokerage firm, you can, of course, ask the firm if it has procedures for beginning an arbitration. If so, try to get the procedures in writing, and in any case you can review any procedures the firm has to see if you find them acceptable. Otherwise, you can contact the various arbitration groups available to you and discuss with them what would be involved in having them arbitrate your claim.

There are a number of things to consider here, including cost, place of arbitration, whether the arbitration would be before one arbitrator or a panel, and whether the arbitration would involve a hearing or just a review of papers submitted. Rather than do all that and make all the decisions on your own, I'd suggest that you talk to a lawyer. It really shouldn't cost much, or perhaps anything, to get some advice on how best to begin an arbitration in your particular situation, and a lawyer could save you from some bad choices.

How long does it take to get through an arbitration proceeding?

In the simplest arbitrations, everything should be finished in less than six months. Even the most complex arbitrations usually can be completed within no more than a year to a year and a half.

What are my chances of winning an arbitration?

If you have a good case, you have a very good chance of winning the arbitration, provided your case is well presented. Virtually all arbitrators try to be fair, and most know what they are doing. They usually can spot cases where a broker or brokerage firm has violated duties to an investor. The sad thing is that investors have to go to the expense and trouble of arbitration to get such cases resolved.

Part V

WHAT
DOES . . . MEAN?

The idea behind this part of the book is to give you the basic meanings of terms used in the book. The descriptions of terms contained here are not meant to be full or technical definitions; in most cases, the definitions are based on those in the text, usually at the first appearance of the word or phrase. Thus, if you have read the book straight through to this point and have a good enough memory, you probably do not need this glossary. If you are dipping into the book, I hope these definitions will be of help.

Glossary

Affiliate A person who either controls, is controlled by, or is under common control with another person. Whether an investor is an affiliate of a company usually comes down to whether the investor is one of a group of persons who control the company, participate in controlling the company, or at least have the power to participate in controlling the company. (Sad to say, the concept of "control" is very tricky.)

American depositary receipts Receipts issued by American banks that evidence an indirect ownership interest in a foreign security that is owned (or at least controlled) by the bank. ADRs let investors easily "own" securities issued by other than American or Canadian companies.

Annual report Contains a company's basic financial statements and other information about the company's operations during the previous year. Most companies publish them in the spring.

Back-end load Charges made at the time mutual fund shares are sold, which can run to several percent of the price of the shares.

Bearer bonds Bonds not registered in anyone's name, but rather payable to whoever presents them for payment. Bearer bonds have coupons attached that are clipped and presented for payment whenever interest payments are due, usually semi-annually.

Beneficial owner The real owner of a security. He or she is shown as owner of the security on the books of his or her brokerage firm, but not on the books of the company that issued the security, unless the beneficial owner is also the record owner.

Blue chip stocks An informal label for stock of a stable, old-line company that offers investors a relatively safe investment. The label comes from the color of the poker chip with the highest value, and more generally means a valuable asset.

Boiler room The securities industry's equivalent of a den of thieves, all huddled together in one room and talking on telephones to prospective victims.

Bona fide purchaser An innocent purchaser who has taken securities without notice of a problem in the title to the securities.

Bond Corporate bonds are usually long-term debt instruments (often not due to be paid for twenty or thirty years) that are issued under the terms of an indenture and secured by a mortgage or deed of trust on corporate property. Government bonds are long-term debt instruments that are much like corporate bonds, but they are not issued under the terms of an indenture, and they typically are not secured by specific property.

Broker The term "broker" means both the firm that helps investors buy and sell securities that are owned by other people and the person at that firm with whom investors do business.

Brokerage firm So far as the ordinary investor is concerned, a brokerage firm is a company that helps the investor buy and sell securities. Brokerage firms perform many other functions and operate in a variety of ways, often adopting a different title (for example, investment bank or investment banking firm) for the different function.

Call The contractual right to buy a given amount of a particular security at a specified price.

Callable A callable security is one that can be paid off, before maturity if the security has a maturity, by the company that issued it.

Cash account The type of account most customers have with a brokerage firm. With a cash account, you have to pay cash for most securities purchased within five business days.

Cash dividend From an investor's standpoint, a cash dividend is a payment by a corporation in cash to its shareholders, the amount of which is so much per share owned. In some states, the dividend may be paid from capital contributed to the corporation, which can have some tax consequences, at least at the federal level. That payment often is more properly called a "distribution" under corporation law.

Certificate of deposit A certificate indicating that a given amount of money has been deposited at the bank that issued the certificate.

Churning Trading for a customer's account for the purpose of generating commissions for the broker rather than profit for the customer.

Class action A lawsuit that is brought on behalf of not only the named plaintiff but everyone else similarly situated.

Client agreement The client agreement, or a document with a similar title, is what brokerage firms ask new clients to sign when they set up an account. It is long, detailed, and filled with fine print.

Closed-end mutual fund A closed-end fund registers with the SEC only a specified number of shares that the fund wishes to sell to the public. When those shares have been sold, the fund is considered closed, and, after that time, the only way you can buy shares in the fund is to buy them in the trading market, just the way you buy shares of stock.

Common stock The basic ownership interest in a corporation. Typically, the owners of a corporation's common stock elect directors, vote on changes to the corporation's charter, have a right to receive all dividends declared by the board of directors (after any dividends on any preferred stock have been paid), and have a right to receive the corporation's assets (after creditors and preferred shareholders have been paid) if the corporation is liquidated.

Confirmation You should receive a confirming telephone call from your broker the same day you make a trade. In that call, the broker can be expected to pass on the price at which the securities were bought or sold, along with the total amount you owe in the case of a purchase. In addition, a written confirmation should be mailed within a day or two after an order is executed.

Control security A security that is owned by an affiliate of the company that issued the security.

Convertible A security that can under specified circumstances, at the option of the owner, be converted into another kind of security.

Coupon rate The interest rate that is specified on a bond. The term comes from bearer bonds, which actually have coupons to clip.

Current yield The return on a bond an investor can get currently, in terms of interest, relative to the current market price of the bond.

Daisy chain A series of trades in a security at successively higher or lower prices, typically with the connivance of a market maker, intended to drive the price of the security up or down, whichever best fits the market manipulator's scheme.

Day order An order to buy or sell a security that expires at the end of the trading day if it hasn't been executed. Market orders are generally understood to be day orders.

Dealer To the securities industry, a "dealer" is a brokerage firm when it buys and sells securities for its own account, taking title itself when it buys securities from an investor and passing title to an investor when it sells.

Debenture In general financial parlance, a debenture is much like a corporate bond, except that debentures are not secured by any property. They are, however, typically issued under an indenture, just the way bonds are. Debentures typically have shorter terms than do bonds.

Debt security A security, such as a bond, that makes the holder of the security a creditor of a company.

Depository Trust Company A company that holds title to securities for securities firms and other institutions.

Discount firm Discount firms do little or nothing more than buy and sell securities for customers. With such limited services, they can afford to charge much lower commissions than full-service firms.

Discount on a bond A bond selling at less than par value, usually $1,000, is said to be selling at a discount.

Discretionary account An account with a brokerage firm that allows a broker to make buy-and-sell decisions for a customer on his or her own.

Dividend-reinvestment plan A plan established by a publicly held company that allows shareholders automatically to buy shares of the company's stock with their dividends.

Equity security A security that represents the interest of an owner in a company.

Exchange offer In an exchange offer, a company goes to the holders of a particular type of security, typically preferred stock, and offers to exchange that security for some other security.

Ex-dividend date The date on and after which the purchaser of shares will not have the right to receive the next dividend payment. Traditionally, it is four business days prior to the record date.

Exempt offering An offering of securities that are exempt from the registration requirements of the securities laws.

Financial plan A listing of where you expect to get funds from and what you expect to do with them.

Financial planner Someone who develops financial plans.

Form 10-K A report that is required to be filed annually by publicly held companies with the SEC. The report, which typically is filed every March, contains a detailed description of the company and its activities.

Front-end load A sales commission payable upon the purchase of shares in a mutual fund.

Full-service firm A firm that provides all the services typically offered by brokerage firms.

Good-until-cancelled order A buy or sell order that stays in effect until you cancel it or until it is executed (although, as a practical matter, brokerage firms may set limits on how long they are willing to keep orders on their books).

In-and-out trading The classic trading pattern in churning, where a customer's account is rarely left alone for any long period.

Income bond A bond on which the interest is payable only if the company has earnings out of which the interest can be paid.

Indenture A contract between a corporation that is issuing securities (almost always bonds or debentures) and a trustee (usually a bank) acting for the benefit of the security holders. The indenture will contain provisions that require the corporation to do certain things and refrain from certain other things. During the life of the security, the trustee monitors the corporation's acts to see it is in compliance with the terms of the indenture. If it is not, the trustee can take the corporation to court in an attempt to protect the interests of the security holders.

Intrastate offering An offering that is made only to persons who are "residents" of a state or territory of which the issuer of the security is also a "resident" of and in which the issuer does at least the bulk of its business.

Investment adviser Someone who either makes specific recommendations on what securities to buy and sell or who buys and sells for you. Also called a "money manager."

Joint tenancy A form of joint ownership of property in which the survivor takes ownership to the whole property (such as a brokerage account) automatically upon the death of the other joint tenant. Sometimes abbreviated as JTWROS or JTROS.

Junk bond A bond that has high risk and pays high interest.

Leveraged buyout (LBO) In an LBO, a company's management, or some outside firm that may or may not have the cooperation of management, takes over a company, usually by means of a tender offer, and borrows massively to finance the buyout.

Limit order In a limit order, you give your broker the maximum price you will pay if you are buying or the minimum price you will take if you are selling.

Load mutual fund A type of mutual fund that has a front-end load of between 3 percent and 8.5 percent.

Low-load mutual fund A type of mutual fund that has a front-end load of less than 3 percent.

Maintenance requirement A requirement that at all times you must have equity in a margin account that is equal to at least a specified percentage of the then current market value of the stocks in the account.

Margin account An account with a brokerage firm in which the firm extends you credit so that you can buy stocks partially on credit.

Margin requirement Under the Securities Exchange Act of 1934, the Federal Reserve Board sets the percentage of borrowed money that can be used to purchase or carry securities. The Board's regulation T governs loans from brokerage firms (other regulations cover other borrowing situations) and currently allows investors to borrow up to 50 percent of the cost of the securities.

Market maker A dealer, operating in the over-the-counter market, that maintains an inventory of a particular company's securities and holds itself out as being willing, on a continuing basis, to buy and sell those securities.

Market manipulation Essentially, anything done to increase or decrease the price of a security artificially.

Market order An order to buy or sell "at the market." That means that the order is to be put through at the best price obtainable, during the normal trading session, when the order hits the trading floor, in the case of exchange-traded securities, or when your brokerage firm can accomplish the transaction in the over-the-counter market.

Mark-up The amount a market maker adds to the price it is paying for a security in the market on the sale of that security.

Matched order The purchase and sale of the same security, at the same time, through different brokerage firms. The idea is to create apparent trading activity at prices essentially set by the trader.

Material information In the context of buying or selling a security, information is material if there is a substantial likelihood that a reasonable investor would attach importance to it in determining whether to purchase or sell the security.

Merger In legal terms, corporations may merge by following the requirements specified in the relevant state corporation statute, usually including specified votes by the boards of directors and shareholders of each corporation entering into the merger. When corporations merge, one of them survives and the other or others go out of existence. The surviving corporation takes all the assets and liabilities of the other corporation or corporations that entered into the merger.

Municipal bond A bond issued by a governmental entity at the state or local level, not necessarily — or even commonly — by a municipality. "Munis" vary in whether or not they are backed by the taxing power of the issuer and whether or not they are free from federal, state, or local taxation.

Mutual fund A company that takes in money from investors and then invests that money in stocks, bonds, or other securities. By owning a mutual fund share, what the individual investor really owns, indirectly, is a small piece of all the securities that the mutual fund owns. Another term for a mutual fund is "investment company."

NASDAQ The National Association of Securities Dealers Automated Quotation system, which is a computerized trading system in the over-the-counter market.

National Association of Securities Dealers, Inc. An association to which virtually all brokerage firms belong and which has power, under federal law, to regulate the activities of brokerage firms and the brokers who work for them.

No-load mutual fund A type of mutual fund that has no front-end load.

Nonretail firm A securities firm that does no retail business, but rather sells securities mostly to institutions, such as insurance companies and pension funds, or wholesales securities to retail firms. In addition, nonretail firms service a fairly small number of wealthy individual investors.

Note In financial terms, a note is a debt instrument, whether secured or unsecured. Notes are almost never issued under indentures the way bonds and debentures are. Also, notes are generally for much shorter terms than are bonds or debentures.

Open-end mutual fund An open-end mutual fund has no set number of shares that it will issue. Rather, it registers with the SEC, from time to time, whatever number of shares it believes it may be able to sell in the foreseeable future. Investors always can buy shares in an open-end fund directly from the fund itself.

Option A right to purchase some other security of the corporation that granted the option. The terms "option" and "warrant" are synonymous.

Over-the-counter market The way securities that are not listed on an exchange are sold through securities firms acting as dealers. The term comes from the fact that, in a sense, securities firms sell securities directly to investors in the same sort of way that stores sell merchandise "over the counter."

Par value (bonds) Bonds are almost always issued in denominations of $1,000 or a multiple thereof. The par value of such a bond is said to be $1,000.

Par value (stock) A dollar figure, specified in a corporation's charter, from which various consequences flow at state law.

Penny stock A stock that originally sells for less than $5 (and often less than $1) and that is issued by a small company with prospects that are, at best, uncertain.

Ponzi scheme One type of pyramid scheme. In a Ponzi scheme, at least some money from later investors is used to pay off earlier investors, thus hiding the fact that the scheme is a fraud and allowing the perpetrators of the scheme to keep it alive.

Post The place on the floor of a stock exchange where particular securities trade.

Preferred stock Stock that is preferred over a corporation's common stock in some way or other. Although it is technically an equity security (that is, it represents an ownership interest in the company), in practical terms preferred stock in a publicly held corporation usually seems more like a debt security, such as a bond.

Premium on a bond Any price in excess of the bond's par value, usually $1,000.

Private placement An exempt offering of securities under section 4(2) of the Securities Act of 1933. Usually, private placements are offerings to institutional investors or wealthy and sophisticated private investors.

Prospectus A specialized document that describes securities being sold and the company selling them.

Proxy A document that authorizes one or more other people to vote shares for their owner.

Proxy fight A proxy fight occurs when competing groups, one of them usually the corporation's management, engage in an information war trying to get shareholders to sign proxies sent by the group.

Proxy statement A document sent to shareholders in publicly held companies whenever their votes are solicited in connection with a shareholders' meeting.

Put A contractual right to sell a specified amount of a given security at a particular price.

Pyramid scheme A pyramid scheme works on the same principle as a chain letter. The first persons in the scheme get money from people they bring in, who are supposed to recruit others into the scheme to pay money to others higher up in the scheme, and so on over and over again.

Record date Typically, in corporations that pay dividends, the board of directors will declare the dividends payable to all shareholders whose names appear on the company's books as shareholders at the close of business on a certain date in the future, which is called the "record date."

Record owner The record owner of a security is the owner shown on the books of the company that issued the security.

Registered bond A registered bond, like common or preferred stock, is registered on the books of the issuer in the name of the owner.

Registered public offering In a registered public offering, a company registers with the SEC, and state securities agencies, securities that it or one or more of its major shareholders wishes to sell.

Regulation A offering An offering that follows the requirements of regulation A under the Securities Act of 1933. That means it is generally for less money and with somewhat lesser requirements than a registered public offering. Nevertheless, despite being an exempt offering, to the average investor it looks like a registered public offering. So much is that the case that traditionally a regulation A offering has been called by those in the securities industry a short-form registration.

Regulation D offering An exempt offering of securities allowed by regulation D under the Securities Act of 1933.

Regulation T The regulation of the Federal Reserve Board that sets the margin requirement in existence from time to time for loans from brokerage firms. Currently regulation T allows a margin account investor to borrow up to 50 percent of the cost of stocks purchased for the account.

Restricted security An investor gets restricted securities if he or she acquired those securities directly or indirectly from the issuer, or from an affiliate of the issuer (or, in certain circumstances, even from a private investor), not in the trading market but in any of a number of types of transactions that are exempt from the registration requirements of the Securities Act of 1933.

Retail firm Retail brokerage firms are the firms that the average investor is likely to be most familiar with, since they are the firms that have storefront offices and that advertise for business from the general public.

Rights offering In a rights offering, a company makes an offer to each of its shareholders to sell to them a certain number of shares of the company's stock at a specified price.

Round lot On at least the New York and American Stock Exchanges, stock trades in 100-share lots, and so, if you trade 100 shares or a multiple of 100, you are trading in a round lot or lots. With a few exceptions, any trade of fewer than 100 shares is an odd lot, and you will have to pay what is called an odd-lot differential for each share you purchase in an odd lot. Typical round lots for bonds are $1,000 and $100,000 in face value.

Rule 701 offerings Rule 701 offerings are offering made, in accordance with rule 701 under the Securities Act of 1933, to employees, officers, directors, or certain other people having close relationships with a privately owned company.

Scalping In a scalping scheme, a brokerage firm itself buys securities in a relatively small company whose stock is traded in the over-the-counter market. Then the firm has its brokers recommend the purchase of that same security to a large number of customers. As those customers purchase the securities, the market price will be driven up by the artificially created demand. The brokerage firm then sells its securities at a profit and stands on the sidelines watching the market price decline after the artificially created demand has stopped.

Security holder's proposal Under the SEC's rule 14a-8, management is required to include in its proxy statement proposals made by security holders, along with limited supporting statements, when certain conditions are met.

Self-regulatory organization An organization, such as a stock exchange, that is given power, under federal law, to regulate its own affairs under the supervision of the SEC.

Selling short Selling short means you sell securities at a time when you either do not own those securities or, even though you own them, you are not able to, or do not wish to, sell the securities you own. The latter situation is known in the industry as selling short "against the box."

Settlement date The date upon which payment must be made for securities that are purchased.

Short-swing trading provisions Basically, section 16(b) of the Securities Exchange Act of 1934 provides that if any profit is made, by a person who is subject to its provisions, on any purchase and sale or sale and purchase of any equity security issued by the person's company, then the profit is to be paid over to the company if the transactions occurred within less than six months of each other. Persons who under federal law are considered to be officers, directors, or owners of more than 10 percent of an equity security of a publicly held company are subject to the short-swing trading provisions.

Sinking fund for bonds Under the terms of some bonds, the company that issues the bonds must set aside in a special account a specified amount of money each year in order to ensure that funds will be available to repay the bonds at their maturity.

Specialized firm Brokerage firm that provides more or less full services, but with respect to only some kinds of securities.

Stock dividend The mechanics of declaring and paying a dividend in a corporation's own stock are essentially the same as for a cash dividend. The corporation might, for example, declare and pay a 5 percent stock dividend on its common stock. What would happen is that each shareholder would receive five additional shares for each one hundred previously owned.

Stock exchange Stock exchanges are organizations that provide a marketplace for buying and selling securities. Although they typically are called stock exchanges, many other kinds of securities, such as bonds and stock options, are traded there.

Stock power A form that authorizes the transfer of a security.

Stock split In a stock split, a corporation takes the proper legal action to divide its existing shares into a greater number of shares.

Stop-limit order A stop-limit order combines aspects of the limit order and the stop order. It is an order to buy or sell a security, at a price that you set, once a trade has occurred at or beyond a certain price, which may or may not be the same as the purchase or sale price you have specified. If the securities cannot then be purchased or sold at the price you have set, or a better price, the order will not be executed.

Stop order A stop order, sometimes called a stop-loss order, is an order to buy or sell a security, at the market price, when the security has traded at or beyond the price you specify. That price is called a "stop price."

Straddle A contract that contains both a put and a call for the same security.

"Street name" Taking securities in "Street name" means that the securities will not have your name on them as the owner, but rather they will be in the name of your brokerage firm or some other entity.

Tenancy in common A form of joint ownership of property. When one tenant in common dies, his or her ownership interest in the property, such as a brokerage account, passes to his or her heirs under the terms of a will or state law. The ownership interest does not automatically pass to the surviving owner of the account.

Tender offer Neither the SEC nor the courts have decided on an exact definition of a tender offer. From the viewpoint of the average investor in the typical tender offer, however, a tender offer looks like this: a company announces publicly that it will buy some or all of the shares of another company's stock in exchange for cash, shares of stock in the offering company, or some combination. The offer to buy will always be at a premium over the current market price of the target company's stock. Typically, the offer is made contingent upon the offering company's being able to purchase a set percentage of the target's stock, such as a majority. Typically, also, the offer will be open only for a limited period of time.

Tender offer (friendly) A tender offer in which the management of the target company goes along with the tender offer rather than fights it.

Tender offer (hostile) A tender offer in which the management of the target company fights the tender offer.

Term insurance With term life insurance, the money you spend goes only to provide insurance coverage, and the policy, therefore, never builds up any cash value.

Tie-in sale Tie-in sales occur in registered public offerings. In this scheme, a brokerage firm requires someone purchasing securities in a public offering to agree subsequently to purchase additional securities, at a higher price, in the trading market.

Tombstone advertisement Advertisement for securities that are in a stylized format reminiscent of a tombstone.

Transfer agent A bank that handles the mechanics of stock transfers for the company that issues the securities.

Treasury bonds, Treasury notes, and Treasury bills There are other differences between these U.S. government securities, such as the minimum denominations available for each, but the overwhelmingly important difference is their maturity. Treasury bills mature in either three months, six months, or one year; Treasury notes mature in from two to ten years; and Treasury bonds have maturities of over ten years, with the maximum being thirty years. All of these securities are backed by what is called the "full faith and credit" of the U.S. government.

Underwriter In financial parlance, a securities firm that helps a company, or its major shareholders, sell securities to the public through an offering that is registered under the federal securities laws. Under the securities law, an individual can meet the technical definition of "underwriter," and securities firms can meet that definition in other than registered public offerings.

Warrant A right to purchase some other security of the corporation that granted the warrant. The terms "option" and "warrant" are synonymous.

Wash sale In a wash sale, a person or firm purchases and sells the exact same securities at the same time through the same brokerage firm. What that does is create apparent activity in the trading of the stock, which has a tendency to drive up the price of the stock in the market.

Williams Act Federal legislation, which added and amended a number of sections to the Securities Exchange Act of 1934, that regulates tender offers.

Wrap fee A fee, paid to a brokerage firm, that covers both investment advisory and brokerage fees.

Yield to maturity of a bond The yield to maturity of a bond is the rate of return an investor will receive, on average, if the bond is held from the date of purchase to the date of maturity.

Zero-coupon bond A zero-coupon bond is a bond that does not pay any interest.

Index

F

G

Information
    about companies invested in, 155–57
    materially false, 198–99
    misleading, 198–99
    proxy statements, 160
    requirements
        opening brokerage account, 37–39
        private placements, 119
        regulation D offerings, 120
    tipping material inside, 189, 191
    trading in possession of material inside, 189
Initial public offerings (IPOs), 105–06, 109, 111–12
Inside information
    tipping material, 189, 191
    trading in possession of material, 189
Insider
    defined, 189–90
    trading, 99–100, 105, 189–93, 196, 206
Institutional investors
    generally, 30, 79–79
    lending securities for selling short, 97
Insurance
    agents as financial planners, 9
    as investment vehicle, 63–67
    brokerage accounts, 57
    certificates of deposit, 67–68
    commissions for financial planners, 10
    company selection, 66–67
    policies, 7
    protecting investors, 217
Integrity of brokers, 34–35, 37
Interest
    accrued on bonds, 135

Replacing securities certificates, 144-45
Reports of
    research, 104
    stock prices, 157
Repurchases of stock, 176-78
Requesting action by directors, 162
Requirements
    duty not to trade under rule 10b-5, 190
    financial planners (legal), 8
    listing securities on exchange, 84
    margin, 67
    open brokerage account, 37-39
Resale limitations on securities
    generally, 179-86
    held by affiliates, 185
    restricted, 119-20, 123-25
Research function of brokerage firms, 29, 32-33, 103-04, 155
Residents of single state, 121
Response to perceived victimization (stepped), 219
Restricted securities
    defined, 180-81, 254
    generally, 180-83
    legended, 124
    resale limitations, 119-20, 123-25
Restrictions on
    intrastate offerings, 123
    selling short, 99
    short-swing trading, 187-89
    trading by insiders, 99-100
Retail brokerage firms
    defined, 254
    generally, 30
Retirement plans, 160

S

W

Y

Z